RADIO SILENCE

JOEL A. CAPELL

I would like to thank
those who were there with me.

To an even greater extent I'd like to thank
those who were there for me.

When life commands
that your bags may not be unpacked…
…may your load be light.

CONTENTS

ABOUT THE AUTHOR (and his doppelganger, a military clone)

Joel A. Capell was born in 1976 in the rural Ohio town of Willard. His military career began with the United States Army Engineers in 1995. He obtained his baccalaureate degree in 2000 from Wittenberg University in Springfield, Ohio, where he studied Computer Graphics and Sociology. Joel's literary works include a few First United Methodist Church Bulletins, a dozen or so Wittenberg Torch campus newspaper sarcasms, and now "Radio Silence".

Mr. Capell or Joel as he would prefer, has maintained a civilian career and has honorably executed his military obligations for the U.S. Army for over half of his lifetime. Having these dual roles for many years is how his military doppelganger, Sergeant Capell, fits into the picture.

Joel's military doppelganger, Sergeant First Class Capell is a twenty-four year and counting U.S. Army veteran. Sergeant Capell has been deployed on three separate yearlong tours in support of the Global War on Terrorism. While serving as an Engineer in 2003-2004 he assisted with the construction of a bridge, a Tactical Operations Center (TOC) and with clearing too many to count Improvised Explosive Devices (IED's) from the streets of Iraq. Sergeant Capell is currently deployed to the Middle East, serving another yearlong tour as a logistician with a Sustainment Brigade. He is expected to return home safely to his wife Jennifer and their family of four children soon.

Sergeant Capell has been to Panama in support of Operation New Horizons, and to Germany in support of dark beer drinking while on illusory Operation Nearly Horizontal, during Oktoberfest. He has also been to Texas, because nearly everyone who has made even a partial career in the U.S. Army has been to Texas. Sergeant Capell has earned twenty one military service medals including a Meritorious Service Medal, two Army Commendation Medals, a German Armed Forces Proficiency Badge, a Combat Action Badge and two Meritorious Unit Citations.

While Sergeant Capell has served his country honorably, Joel has had an extensive list of civilian careers including summer lifeguard and swimming lessons coach, dish washer at the Delta Gamma sorority house while in college, custom home builder, hardware store manager, facilities maintenance manager, military fleet manager, and is currently partnered in two Limited Liability Companies (LLC's). He, his wife Jennifer, their Rottweiler Desi-Lou, and their ten chickens are the managing members of "Rush Creek Financial", where they offer clients insurance and tax services, investments, financial planning, and farm fresh eggs. Their second LLC, "Rush Creek Homes" is an investment and long term property management company, providing affordable housing for families in their rural Ohio community.

Soon after Sergeant Capell returns from his current deployment, Joel may once again be found at one of his children's sporting events, shooting guns on Grandad's farm, or on a motorcycle ride with his wife. The "Mouser Capell Motorcycle Club of Mount Victory" ("MCMC Mt.V"), is the author's motorcycle club. Joel had always dreamed of being a member of a motorcycle gang, so he created one. "MCMC Mt.V" has its own logo consisting of a colorful rooster perched upon a hog. Not a motorcycle "hog", but a bacon hog. The club also has a single Christmas tree ornament and eight current members. They are, however, expected to have an outstanding year of growth due to the publishing of "Radio Silence".

Roosters and Christmas tree ornaments are not the ingredients of a Hells Angels biker, but if you would like to be a proud rooster on a hog, T-shirt wearing "MCMC Mt.V" member, please contact the author, also club president. Joel would be more than happy to oblige your request in-between puttering around his home or at one of his Rush Creek properties, where generally, he engineers excuses to wear a tool belt. "MCMC Mt.V" would be delighted to have you aboard.

Joel, his doppelganger, and his family are extremely excited about "Radio Silence". They hope you will enjoy the read, and always enjoy the ride.

Author, in Kuwait Feb. 2018
Wearing his "MCMC Mt.V" T-shirt

RADIO SILENCE

Twelve weeks or so into the war I fought in Iraq, I was a part of a small convoy on the way to FOB (Forward Operating Base) Warrior, which was in the oil rich region of Kirkuk, Iraq. Just over the crest of a mild gradient hill I could see signs of a small village off in the distance. The hillside stretched out in a gradual downward direction for about two miles. Due to the mostly barren and rural landscape, vision was never an issue in Iraq. There was literally nothing out there to interfere with line of sight. In fact, I will probably never see more stars in the sky than on those nights I was in the Iraqi countryside at midnight.

Protocol for entering a populated area was to maintain radio silence. Maintaining our own silence allowed for acute listening for signs of disturbance. Communication radio speakers inside most vehicles were maxed out, just in case the time came when everyone needed to be able to hear commands over the firing of our mounted weapons systems overhead.

Radio silence was quite comforting while entering a quaint little village. It was also comforting, knowing that I was nearly certain to make some child's day by tossing him or her some peanut butter and candy from a MRE (Meal Ready to Eat). Nearly every vehicle had a box of goodies, which were saved for such occasions.

In addition to the candies, I was currently prepared to toss out my very first soccer ball to a group of unsuspecting children. I had ordered twenty soccer balls from Amazon.com, and had them shipped to me the second month I was in Iraq. Every surrounding village had a minimum of two new soccer balls when I left. They brought many delighted smiles to both children and soldier alike. Even during times of war, good people somehow find good things to help them keep their sanity.

Moving along in our vehicles at about 30 mph, everything we could see had a mid-grade brown hue to it. Everything on this hillside was flat, sandy dirt, and rock. About 700 meters from us, in the two o'clock direction was a twisting tornado dust devil, extending upward infinitely into the sky.

The she-devil was quite a beautiful spectacle to behold in our sore and tired eyes. Her enchanting dance reminded me of a cobra snake, under the spell of her charmer's flute. She danced around shaking her hips slowly back and forth over the barren landscape. Every few seconds an arm of dust would extend in a quick offshoot and then whip back into her body. We were mesmerized by her movements.

She was a nonviolent natural beauty on a scale of heavenly proportion. She moved provocatively closer to our line of slow moving vehicles. I am certain if Ali Baba snuck up on us from the seven o'clock direction, he could have stolen everything we had. Not a single eye in that convoy was focused anywhere but on the belly dancing she-devil at our two o'clock.

She triumphed in her intention to get closer to us, as we all subconsciously invited her in. Soon she danced her way onto the road with our convoy. Her tail twisted around below her hips and was sucked into the vacuum created by the lead vehicle of our convoy, which was directly in front of mine. Her tail latched on and engulfed the entire vehicle. She guided our expedition on its present course, from the very front of our convoy, for the next sixty seconds.

Seconds before she whipped off the vehicle and followed the course that nature had intended, Specialist Jake, his lower lip filled with Copenhagen, broke the protocol of radio silence from the vehicle being engulfed by the dancing she-devil.

Muffled by the whirlwind, everyone heard Jake's crackling voice over their own vehicle's internal communication speakers. "Toto, I don't think we're in Kansas anymore."

Not another word was spoken. Radio silence...

DEAR JENNIFER,

When I started writing these memoir letters many years ago the only thing I didn't have was an actual name to whom I could tell these stories. I was missing that special someone to address. In fact, the original title to "Radio Silence" was, "Dear _____, this is How I Got Here". Even back then I knew you would one day walk into my life and I wanted to be capable of effectively communicating these stories when you did finally arrive. I am thankful every single day that the blank space in the original title has been filled by you, the greatest woman on the planet. These letters have always been written to you, Jennifer. You just hadn't fit snugly into your spot next to me at their inception.

It has taken me nearly ten years to compile these letters home into "Radio Silence". They are a conglomeration of stories capturing my years spent overseas in support of the War on Terror. They also describe the years of struggle and the war within my own head afterwards.

Many of the stories had to be meticulously unearthed over time. Negotiating a contract to reopen the memories involving my most unnerving skeletons was difficult. A few of those skeletons in my closet are found within the darkest period of my life, when I lived as a homeless man in a Volunteers of America veteran's shelter in Columbus, Ohio. The 45 days prior to being homeless was rock bottom for me, the worst days of my life.

Some of these letters are certainly written with an overabundance of sarcasm. Veterans are extremely sarcastic people. "Embrace the suck" is a well-known sarcastic saying among soldiers, and we believe in that embracement whole heartedly. We learn to wrap our minds around things that may seem horrible to "normal" or non-military folks. The process of embracing the suck in order to survive our sometimes drastic life situations is how military members endure. Thus, our sarcasm is born.

It is quite true that I have learned to deal with some abnormal experiences as a direct result of being a soldier. In fact, Jennifer, the entire reason that I have written you these letters over the years is because I have experienced abnormality. Most people, you included, would never have pondered the things you will read about here. But like any soldier, I have embraced the suck to the best of my ability and continue along my journey.

I've found that sarcasm can sometimes be difficult to express on paper. But as a veteran, sarcasm will forever remain a part of who I am. For instance, it may seem from my writings that I have an extreme dislike for the Army. But I do not hate the Army. I hate the suck that the Army sometimes brings us, but I embrace it. "Us" encompasses both soldiers and their spouses. Spouses, you included, are naturally pulled into that embrace as well.

Overall, I've loved my extensive and successful military career. I volunteered for it, and have had the privilege of serving our great country for 24 years, and counting. Obviously, I don't hate it... all the time.

Because of years of juggling military hardships along with life's normal idiosyncrasies, very few things are immune to a veteran's sarcasm. Veterans will literally make fun of everything. You will read stories about how the Army has to some extent transformed me into a sarcastic dark humorist, and a hardened individual. I personally still hold a few things sacred and untouchable, but many veterans will pluck any sacred fruit from the tree and make fun of it. Ill-timed and dark humor is a result of constantly embracing the suck.

Veterans will absolutely make fun of everything, including one another. It's one of our favorite pastimes. I fully expect that after laying my life out on these pages, I will be made fun of. As a veteran I am fine with that. I can, and will laugh with my fellows at my own shortcomings. Constantly embracing the suck creates individuals with thick skin and broad shoulders.

At no time during reading should a conclusion be made that I am somehow a victim. I am not a victim of others, of circumstance, of Veterans Affairs (VA) healthcare, of war, or of anything else for that matter. Circumstances, the VA, and war happen to be parts of my story, or parts of the life I chose. The only thing I may be a victim of is simply being human. I have made some poor decisions while learning how to cope with life to the best of my ability. If to ere is human, I am certainly human. I take complete responsibility for my actions, and do not insist I am owed anything because of my struggles. From the painted picture within these memoirs, the takeaway should not be of me as a victim. But only that these hardships were, and are a part of my life.

These letters are aimed at letting me introduce each skeleton in my closet to you, and allowing you to shake hands with them one at a time. Writing has allowed me to carefully reopen each skeleton's respective manila folder. Each folder, had been buried deep within the doldrums of my cobwebbed mind. By putting thoughts to paper I have been able to come to terms with my skeletons and have gained some self-understanding. In addition, I have an interesting avenue to introduce my skeletons to you.

While appreciating their therapeutic consequences I have also had a lot of fun writing these letters. Humorous stories are certainly found tangled within them, but truly they are about losing myself, losing everything, finding you, and finding myself for a second time. They are about life.

Most of the names are changed to protect identity, and a few of the inconsequential specifics have also been altered. Where someone worked, who was the excellent marksman, or writing some small humorous blurb because it made me laugh, are liberties I have taken.

Other than those insignificant freedoms I have taken as the author, these letters home are 100% truths from the perspective of your husband, ten years in the making. And nearly all of these pages were literally written from 6700 miles away while I was deployed. They really are letters home, letters to you.

Someday, others may read them, but their purpose will never change. From their inception these letters have always been written to you.

Dear Jennifer, this is how I got here.

I

Learning to Walk

THE IDEA to write this specific story came to me by way of my children. Isaac was twelve years old when he reminded his Father about this story. I have told it to him a few times over the years. Isaiah, ten at the time, confirmed that he "liked this story too, Daddy."

Jennifer, the following is a story from my own childhood about pressing the limits. It's a theme found throughout "Radio Silence" and throughout my life. This particular story is brought to you by my own children.

A STORY FOR ISAAC & ISAIAH

Growing up in the rural, north central Ohio town of Willard was quite pleasant for me. The 1980's were pleasant for everyone in the Capell household. My parents, both University of Otterbein graduates, had worked very hard to afford us certain luxuries. A beautiful home on the water and an annual two week summer vacation were among the many. During our vacations we visited places like New Orleans LA., Destin FL. and the Black Hills of South Dakota. The remainders of our summers were filled with more vacation like days. Those days were filled with things such as waterskiing and swimming, followed by BBQ and evening bonfires. Fun was a regular and wonderful occurrence in the small community where my younger brother and I grew up. Holiday Lakes, just outside of Willard, Ohio was quite possibly the greatest place on the planet to be a boy.

Holiday Lakes was a neighborhood that really had no boundaries for us as kids. From the lake, to the woods, to the community's yards, the world as we knew it had no fences. Walking through private yards and property that didn't belong to us was never an issue. We were good kids, and for the most part respected what was ours and what was not ours equally. Therefore, we were free to wander the neighborhood, and free to explore and enjoy the woods and streams that housed crawdads and tadpoles.

There were eleven boys within a five mile radius of the Capell home. We could in fact field our own football team. I was the ringleader as the oldest and the largest of the neighborhood boys. On days we weren't in the woods or in the lake swimming, we played football, whiffle ball, ultimate Frisbee, kickball and soccer. We also held World Wrestling Federation (WWF) wrestling matches in a centrally located neighborhood front yard. You name it, we played it.

By the first snow of each year there was barely any grass left in that yard. Months of cleats and wrestling matches mixed with the dry August heat had taken its toll on our playground. The homeowner didn't mind all of us kids tearing up his yard every year, as long as we would help him plant new grass each fall. And we did. In order to play hard we learned that we must also work hard. This life lesson was among the many that we were taught during our young and innocent years.

Both my Mother and Father were always eager to hear about how we had recently improved the defensive fortress that we had built from fallen timbers in the neighborhood woods. And even though Dad had just returned home from a long day of work, he would still make it a point to visit our fortress at least once a week, to see the latest developments we had made. As a young boy, recognition from my Father was exactly what I desired. My brother and I received that often.

The first eighteen years of my life were filled with countless blessings mostly provided by my loving parents. I was lucky to have them then, and am lucky to have them now.

A short aside: I'd like to take a moment to say, thank you Mom and Dad. You did an absolutely fantastic job in what many would deem the most important role of your lives. Nick and I are truly blessed to have you, and because of you.

Back then packing a backpack full of peanut butter and Grandma's strawberry jam sandwiches along with a pocket knife, and riding our bikes into the woods with neighborhood friends for the entire day was commonplace. We built many survival forts out of fallen trees and fought off the imaginary villains lurking among us. We were rarely indoors at all, especially during the summer months. Cell phones and video games had not yet infiltrated the American family's atmosphere.

Things of boyhood dreams such as waterskiing, sledding, gymnastics, strength exercising, and jumping off bridges into the water were the everyday norm at Holiday Lakes. We were always attempting to press the limits and go higher and faster on bike, boat, and foot. One summer we even constructed a BMX bicycle track complete with ramps and banked curves.

My youth consisted of a Boy Scout's paradise by day, completed by a full plate of dinner when my brother and I returned home from our daily adventures. Just like the name states, Holiday Lakes was a place where many people would choose to go while on their holiday. It was a wonderful privilege to have grown up there.

My childhood is filled to the brim with memories that fit into these themes. All of them were made while adventure captured my innocent and constantly wandering boyhood soul.

This particular story about pressing the limits includes the construction of one of our mighty neighborhood tree fortresses, located in a plot of at least one square mile of thick uninhabited woods. The actual property owner may have been known by one of our parents, but was of no consequence to us as children. Property boundaries were seldom drawn, and rarely adhered too.

Our tree fortress was about two miles away from our house when travelling on gravel road. But it was only about fifty feet as the crow flies across the water at the mouth of a cove. I could literally throw a stone and hit the trees containing our fort, but it was a twenty minute bicycle ride to get to it. My brother and I would travel about a mile down one side of the lake's inlet and another mile back up the other side. Regardless of the distance, we made the trip all the time. Our fortress was the common meeting place, on any afternoon, for all of us boys.

My own Father is still the smartest and handiest man I know. He was the manager of the local hardware store, which was advantageous when it came to construction materials. Back then he would assist us in constructing nearly anything our collective imaginations could come up with. Our imaginations were our greatest tools for adventure, and our only limitation.

With help from Dad and our unrelenting imaginations, we had somehow managed to invent our own functional bungee cord. The contraption consisted of a ski rope handle and an old garage door spring dangling from a branch in an oak tree over the cove of water. Seven, two-foot pieces of 2x4 were attached to the side of the tree trunk with nails. Those steps made a ladder for the twenty foot ascent to the launching platform. From the platform we would jump into the water and then be flung repeatedly back into the warm summer air by the recoiling spring.

We had also constructed a cable zip line that originated from the same platform and spanned the entire fifty feet of cove. Complete with pulley and another old ski rope handle it turned the twenty minute bike ride around the cove into a three second flight to the fortress side of the inlet.

The zip line would easily transport us a single direction down the cable to the opposite shore. However, being an invention that was based purely on the law of gravity, it could not afford us the return trip. We tried and tried again to pull each other back up the cable but never had the strength to manage it. All of our futile attempts ended up with someone splashing wildly into the cool water. We either had to swim home or walk the two mile trek back around the cove after taking the one way flight. One of the neighborhood boys lost his bike in the lake once, after he tried to take it with him across the zip line. His father had to fish it out of ten feet of water with a rope after we failed at several retrieval attempts.

Besides painting a picture of how truly enjoyable my childhood was, the secondary point to this story is to illustrate that even at a very young age, I was a mastermind at "pushing the envelope". I have always had a hunger for pushing the limits. Even today, I still love to press the limits of nearly everything I am involved in. Moderation has never been a well-recognized word in my vocabulary.

My first recollection of pushing the limits is from when I was 3-4 years old. While under my Father's supervision, I'd pound nails into a 2x4 in the garage, concentrating on the task until I was able to pound three in a row without bending one. Then I'd up that number to four in a row and start over.

Very focused, and very driven, working hard to press the limits has been a mantra of mine from the very beginning. During my youth, I'd not just simply go waterskiing, I worked at becoming one of the best slalom skiers on the lake. Later in my life, I became a collegiate athlete by joining the Wittenberg University swim team. There I worked extremely hard to become part of a school record breaking relay team. And eventually, I completely pressed my own limits by joining the Army. Accomplishing, succeeding, always pushing, I have always taken things one step further.

Toward the end of that particular summer, the zip line cable we had looped around the tree and the nails in its trunk had been rather stressful to the ailing oak. It had leaned out over the cove quite a bit more since the zip line's inception. Dad put the rightful kibosh on both the zip line and the bungee cord late that summer, for fear of one of us growing boys being injured. It was only a matter of time before that oak came crashing down.

We were now in need of another way across the cove and I had the perfect solution. On a summer morning like most others, alongside the peanut butter and Grandma's strawberry jam sandwiches in my backpack, I placed a small hatchet. I was going to build a bridge for us.

The base of that old oak tree was at least three feet in diameter, and it would easily span the fifty feet over the cove if felled correctly. I chopped and chipped away at that oak tree for days with my little hatchet. And even though the blisters on my hands bled through my Mother's garden gloves, I never gave up. I was completely focused on a single thing. No matter what it required of me, I was going to build us a bridge. So I packed some gauze pads the next day, put them inside the gloves and kept on chipping.

Finally, after many more days than I expected, that mighty oak tree crashed down to the other shoreline. And I victoriously walked across the trunk to the other side. I had succeeded in making a foot bridge to our fortress. And in my eyes that was the only thing that mattered.

My focused perseverance also came with cases of tunnel vision and other downsides. Sometimes, I was so intent on the goal that I didn't bother looking side to side to see how my actions would impact everything else around me. I did not understand that the entire world was not for my own personal use, and there were in fact boundaries and fences that I should not cross.

In this specific instance, I was so fixated on the construction of a bridge, I had completely missed some of the natural consequences. My new footbridge had blocked several boats located on the inlet's shoreline from rightfully entering the lake. As a consequence of my footbridge and tunnel vision, the local Sheriff showed up at our door a few evenings later. I learned some things about boundaries very quickly while assisting with cleaning up the mess I had created.

Learning from one's mistakes is a lifelong mission. But to this day I have never truly learned the art of moderation. Over the years I have improved, but I'll never master it. It's not in my blood. Something dangerous inside of my head requires me to test the limits of certain situations in order to find the answer to the following question.

What exactly is the breaking point?

JENNIFER, THIS next story gives my insight into why I joined the Army, and also why I chose to attend Wittenberg University.

FINANCING DREAMS

In early 1995 just before high school graduation, like most other eighteen year olds, I was ready to experience a bit of the world outside of my hometown. It was time for me to make some decisions about how I wanted my life to progress. My visions of purchasing a Volkswagen bus and driving aimlessly out to California in search of "the experience" were stomped out before any real consideration. With my current income as a summer lifeguard I couldn't afford a Volkswagen, or any other car for that matter. In retrospect, that beer drinking and occasional pot smoking adventure would have been a horrible idea for me. Needless to say, my parents objected. I wasn't forced to, but I was heavily encouraged to go to college.

As a young man who would be graduating from high school in a few months, I didn't have any money. And I couldn't fathom paying the average of $10,000 dollars a year for tuition. Just turning eighteen, I doubt I had made $10,000 dollars over the course of my entire life. Still living under my parent's roof, I had little concept of money. I knew I wanted to go to college but certainly did not want the burden of paying off years of student loans as part of my future. My parents offered to pay a small portion toward my tuition costs, but I didn't want to place the burden on them either. They had already done so much for me. It was time for me to make my own way.

> Jennifer, I'm sure you remember back then, tuition costs were much cheaper when compared to today's skyrocketing education costs. It gives me nightmares thinking about financing our children's higher education a few years down the road.

I'm not sure if she actually did, but I imagine that my mother shed tears when I told her that an Army Recruiter was going to stop by our house to talk about how the Army could provide 60% of my college tuition costs for four years of college. Her tears may have been proud mama

21

tears because her eldest son had grown into his big boy britches and was making a sound lifelong decision. Or they may have been tears of dear God what did she do wrong to make her oldest child want to go and join the Army? Possibly it was a combination of both.

Most prospective college students take the normal financial route of applying for student loans and grants. Many of them end up obtaining a secondary job in order to pay off their loans. From the hundreds of viable options, most students do find a route to finance their higher education. By joining the Army, I would skip directly over all of these and any other adequate possibilities, and would press the limits on my own route to financing higher education straight to the maximum level.

I weighed my options carefully, through the following thought process.

By joining the Army I would be afforded a concrete plan to go to college that included very "little monetary cost" to myself, and I was quite pleased with that aspect of the decision.

But it was the Army, and what I knew about people in the Army was that they had to go to war. Soldiers fight for freedom, they kill and possibly die and stuff… right? I could in fact die, as a result of this decision. Therefore, a very unpleasant aspect of my financial plan was the possibility of dying for my country. Essentially, joining the Army to finance my education "at little cost", may come "at all costs".

But, then again, it was 1995, and we were not at war. The Cold War with Russia had long been over, and the Vietnam War was years prior to that. The most recent conflict that included the United States was Operation Desert Storm, which lasted what, a week? Also, in six short years I'd have over half of my tuition paid for!

Plus, my recruiter told me, "It was highly unlikely that I'd be called into conflict while I was actively enrolled in college."

Regardless of those facts, less than 2% of the U.S. population have actually joined the military. Most Americans immediately shy away from taking the "at all costs" risk for their country.

I am not most Americans.

The allure and excitement of "at all costs", tugged at my "push the limit" heart strings. With this decision, I would be able to attend college "at little cost" to myself, in exchange for an "at all costs" adventure for my country! As far as I was concerned, joining the Army would be a win, win decision for me.

From the very beginning of my career, including the original decision to enlist, the U.S. Army would be an institution where I could excitedly and effectively test the limits.

Four months prior to my high school graduation I took the Armed Services Vocational Aptitude Battery (ASVAB) test. And I scored very high on the military entrance exam. On February 21st, 1995, with mixed blessings from my parents, I signed a six year enlistment contract with the U.S. Army, specifically the Ohio National Guard. I was going to become a Combat Engineer and learn the engineering arts of construction and demolitions. I would attend Basic Training the September after I graduated high school and forego college for one year in order to have 60% of my annual tuition costs covered.

I didn't know much about the military at all, but with my tunnel vision blinders on I joined the Army to assist with financing the bulk of my college education. And although I didn't know which school I'd be attending yet, a college degree was my goal. I was going to accomplish that goal.

During the summer after my high school graduation, most of my friends left home to begin their own college experience. I helped several of them laboriously move their belongings to their college of choice because I couldn't think of a single reason why I wouldn't want to go hang out at college for a weekend in late summer. Nice weather, girls, beer… why the hell not?

After helping with a few of the moves, the entrepreneur in me thought I could possibly start a business helping young people move to college. Though I supposed not everyone would let me sleep on their couch after the bars closed.

One of the friends that I assisted was moving to Springfield, Ohio, where he would be attending Wittenberg University. Just like the other moves it would consist of a ton of sweaty physical labor in the late August afternoon heat and a couple pick-up trucks, mine included.

Jennifer, that summer I was able to purchase my first pick-up truck because of the money that I had been collecting from the National Guard.

After the "moving to Wittenberg" work for my friend was completed, the ultimate repayment for a young man who was eager to get out of his home town seemed to naturally manifest itself on campus. A reward consisting of a weekend full of parties, a few cold beers and the ever important multitude of college girls!

To make a long story short I spent the 1995 fall semester's opening weekend at Wittenberg. Every single thing about that weekend was absolutely beautiful. I had the time of my life. There were young adults having the times of their lives every direction I turned. Campus was unequivocally magnificent. The architecture was absolutely stunning, there were equally gorgeous young ladies everywhere, and the beers were cold that weekend. Wittenberg University also had a very well respected reputation as an educational institution. Goodness gracious, I was instantly smitten with the entire place.

WITTENBERG UNIVERSITY! GO TIGERS!

I applied for enrollment to the 1996 fall semester after my 1995 opening weekend party adventure, and was accepted. However, there was one obvious drawback to Wittenberg. The annual tuition costs were around $23,000 dollars a year. I would be making the choice to more than double the cost of an average state college if I attended this private institution. A "well respected institution of higher education" mind you. Wittenberg was a great choice for higher education. On the other hand it was possibly a poor choice for financial reasons.

Jennifer, Wittenberg was listed in the Forbes top 25 small universities in the U.S., and to my knowledge remains on that list annually.

But, hadn't I joined the Army to help pay for college? "HOLY SHIT! I JOINED THE ARMY?" I second guessed my own decision when thinking about accepting Wittenberg's offer. What had I done?

"Calm down self! You enlisted in order to help pay for school, therefore you should in fact go to college wherever you truly want to go." I took a moment to consider my recent six year enlistment commitment, and reverted back to my original rationalization to join the Army.

I would attend college at "little cost" to myself, in exchange for the possibility of an "at all costs" adventure, for my country. And my original motive to enlist was to finance my education. So even though tuition there was substantially higher than my other options, I was going to attend Wittenberg University.

That explanation was all the justification I needed to accept Wittenberg's offer. It was a sound decision and my mind was made up. Wittenberg was a choice that I will never, ever regret.

I visited friends at Wittenberg a couple more weekends that fall, before it was time to pay my dues to the U.S. Army and go to Basic Training. As the financier for the excellent education I would receive, the Army would ensure they received their 60% tuition's use out of me.

ALONG WITH my choice to go to Wittenberg, the U.S. Army was another choice that I will never, ever regret.

RULES FOR SMOKING

In late September 1995, I got aboard my very first airplane and flew to Missouri for Basic Training at Fort Leonard Wood. Basic Training, or "Boot Camp", was just like the stories you have no doubt heard, complete with Drill Sergeant's banging trash can lids inches from our heads at 2AM. It was their job to make my life and all the other recruit's lives miserable. Our Drill Sergeants were not just good at their jobs, they were master artists who created devilish and torturous ways to make us miserable. Like screaming bloody murder in our faces while demanding we do absurd amounts of push-ups during frozen "smoking" sessions outside in the snow, while wearing only shorts and shower shoes, commonly known as flip flops.

The U.S. had recently passed a law stating there would be no smoking inside federal buildings, so the Drill Sergeant's took us outside to "smoke". Although Boot Camp was already a tobacco free environment for its recruits, we'd still go outside to "smoke". We recruits, "smoked", by doing sit-ups, push-ups, leg lifters, knee benders, and various other physically exhausting calisthenics exercises. Forced to participate on the unpleasant side of these "smoking" sessions for hours, I would literally steam from the sweat that evaporated off my body in the frigid cold. In actuality, I and all my fellow recruits did appear to smoke. As one large miserably dysfunctional Army family, we all "smoked", together.

Although it's kind of funny just to think about now, I certainly was not laughing at the time. Pain and discomfort ran rampant among us recruits as we rolled around on the wet ground while frigidly "smoking".

Jennifer, I sometimes wonder if some weird word association psychologist recommended that the Army General in charge of Basic Training should refer to the screaming and steaming push-up gatherings as "smoking" sessions. After experiencing these sessions, the mere word "smoking" would cause a nicotine addict to think twice about lighting up again.

We'd go outdoors to "smoke" several times a day no matter what we were in the middle of doing. Every last second of "smoking" was miserable and utterly exhausting. And being a guy who puts all his efforts toward accomplishing the task directly in front of him, I pushed my own limits and was exhausted from day one.

"I'll do your one more push-up, Drill Sergeant!"

There was no way I would allow my Drill Sergeants to get the best of me. They were always demanding more, and soon they knew how many push-ups and sit-ups each of us could actually do. Recruits couldn't occasionally rest by doing fewer repetitions than they were capable.

"I've got two more push-ups for you, Drill Sergeant! Oh, you want three? I got 'em. Bring it! You can't "smoke" a rock, Drill Sergeant!"

No doubt it was miserable, but I curiously excelled at the misery. I know that last statement sounds bizarre but remember that moderation has never been a well-recognized word within my vocabulary. And Boot Camp was anything but moderate.

My current curiosity about how far I could push myself was similar to pounding nails into a 2x4 as a child. Back then, I'd pound three nails in a row without bending one. Then I'd try to up that number to four in a row. During Boot Camp, I did one more push-up until eventually I could do 81 in a row. And then I'd do 82 the next time, maxing out at 87 push-ups in the two minutes we had allotted during our Army Physical Fitness Test (APFT). In some oddball way or another I relished the next challenge at hand and would literally sacrifice myself in order to accomplish it.

The Drill Sergeant's would not beat me, and my own desire to quit wouldn't either. I craved the challenge, and succeeded. Boot Camp transformed me into a physically fit and confident young man. It

27

worked its transformation magic through lessons of discipline and hard work. Boot Camp effectively constructed an ethos for overcoming obstacles in my head. And through determination and perseverance, I realized I could exceed my wildest expectations.

With each new day, I strived to push the limits of yesterday.

More important to this story than "smoking", is that after the entire experience I felt as if I could and would conquer the world if needed. I mean it, I could do anything! I felt there was nothing that life could throw at me that I could not overcome.

The only drawback to the entire confidence building experience was that if I ever was actually going to conquer the world, I'd need a bit of coaxing. I would first need someone to directly articulate what type of _____ (insert expletive) I was, while their forehead blood vessels looked as if they were about to burst an aneurism from underneath a stiff brimmed hat. Secondly, that same individual would have to make some sort of reference to how there was no way in hades that I, "the expletive", could actually conquer the world on my own. And lastly, they would need to scream the direct orders inches from my nose, which told me just how I was in fact going to conquer the world, all due to the fact that their aneurisms had somehow made us all better persons.

Basic Training was a strange psychology experiment. But it was successful on those of us who never gave up.

In addition to the U.S. Army teaching me how to challenge myself and effectively overcome internal and external obstacles, the U.S. Army also taught me how to eat.

During Boot Camp we had limited time to eat before a Drill Sergeant was once again screaming at us to "get up and get out" of the chow hall. I'm not certain I ever tasted anything I ate during my months of not so casual dining at Fort Leonard Wood. Nothing stayed on my tongue long enough to allow my taste buds to register with my brain. That was probably a good thing considering we were eating mostly rice, beans and potatoes, which were all soaked in some sort of powdered flavor packet or canned cafeteria gravy. All of our options were cheap and tasteless calories, made to fuel the warrior masses.

Wait a minute! I misspoke by stating "our options" in the previous sentence. Recruits did not have options. I should have stated all of "them" were cheap and tasteless, and left out "options" altogether. There were no options. If the cooks were serving chili-macaroni, then everyone would receive chili-macaroni. There was no such thing as "special meals" for "special people" back then. No one received special treatment. Everyone ate, breathed, drank, showered, pissed, and shaved (everyone shaved, period) the same. There were no options, and there were no opinions. Everyone did get a participation trophy though. We each received a plate full of chili-macaroni, and around 90 seconds to devour it.

Through all the pain, the overall goal of graduating military Basic Training was accomplished for me and 92 of my fellow Alpha Company, 35th Engineer Battalion classmates. We had started the training with 120 new recruits. Evidently it was an especially tough class. Recruits were "removed" for various reasons, but most often they just couldn't drudge through the day to day misery. They wouldn't press their own limits far enough to make it through, and their minds surrendered to the challenge well before their bodies did.

The graduating "Alpha Assassins" and I were transformed into lean and mean new men. The confidence instilled in us by the U.S. Army was rightfully worn proudly upon our shoulders.

Mom and Dad came to see my Basic Training graduation in March 1996. There never was, and there may never be another time in my life when I was so happy to see my parents. After some long overdue hugs it was finally time go home. We embarked on the twelve hour ride back to hometown Ohio and I fell asleep immediately upon entering the safety of my parent's car. There was still nothing like being under my parent's roof, even if it was the roof of their car.

Over the twelve hour ride home I was awake just long enough to devour a foot long deli sandwich from Subway. It was the best sandwich I have ever eaten, and possibly the only thing I had truly tasted in quite some time. Now having the comfort of my parent's roof and a full stomach, I promptly fell back asleep. I would not wake again until we were in our driveway at Holiday Lakes.

I slept for 11.5 hours… in a car? Boot Camp was exhausting. It was good to be home.

Shortly after returning home from Boot Camp, I got a job at a factory where I worked on a production line making lawnmowers for about six months. The lawnmower production line was definitely not where I wanted to spend the rest of my life. The hatred I held for that factory job reinforced the goal I had set the year prior. I would indeed go to college.

I headed off to Wittenberg that fall, where I'd spend the next four years successfully obtaining my degree.

My freshman year, I joined the varsity swim team. My high school didn't even have a swim team. The only competitive swimming I had ever participated in was a small summer league at the city pool. So why not try out for the collegiate level team? That's a great example of how Boot Camp had morphed me into a bigger competitor, with more confidence, than I had already been. No way would I have fathomed the idea of swimming in college without my newly obtained military mindset.

Through Basic Training, the concept of pressing my own limits had been put on permanent overdrive. I began to wonder, where exactly was my own breaking point?

This is my favorite quote, Jennifer.

Few things are impossible to diligence and skill. Great works are performed not by strength but by perseverance.
- Dr. Samuel Johnson

I continued to press the limits and craved each unique challenge. By doing so I learned that during the course of life's challenges, through perseverance, discipline, and hard work, I would succeed.

THIS IS AN entertaining little story about how I managed to get through my second semester of Spanish while actually being lost in translation.

WHERE HAVE ALL THE LIGHTNING BUGS GONE?

(DONDE SE HAN IDO TODAS LAS LUCIERNAGAS?)

While working toward my degree at Wittenberg I studied diligently. I even pulled a few all-night study sessions, during which I crammed knowledge for tough exams into my head.

Academically, I struggled with my second semester of Spanish more than anything else. My Spanish 200 Professor recognized that I was not doing well in his class and he presented me with a nonstandard idea to assist me through his class. If I agreed to be cast in his production of "Where Have All the Lightning Bugs Gone?", in return I would receive an A+ in Spanish 200 regardless of the actual results of my final exam. It was an offer I couldn't refuse.

"Where Have All the Lightning Bugs Gone?" is a one act play by Louis E. Catron, 1999.

There was, however, a catch to his offer, which would make carrying out his ideas for the production pretty impressive. There would only be two members in the entire cast, so I would be playing the lead male role. And the kicker was that the entire production would be performed in the Spanish language.

What in the hell was my professor thinking? I couldn't speak coherent Spanish, and he knew it! Besides "donde est la cervesa" (where is the beer), I didn't really care to learn. He allegedly chose me because I "had very animated facial features and entertaining responses". What the…?

I accepted his proposal with my blinders on, and didn't really know what I was getting into. However, I did understand that this proposal

31

had a certain "gift" aspect to it. I probably had a better chance of pulling off this theatrical performance than getting a C in Spanish 200. I had to keep a C average in order to keep the Army's tuition benefits and I was not doing very well in his class. He kind of had me by the coconuts, if you know what I mean. It really was an offer I couldn't refuse.

Attempting to learn an hour and ten minutes of dialogue that I really didn't understand was an absolutely grueling chore. The only nice thing about the endeavor was that the star of the show was a very pretty Spanish speaking Latina.

Four nights a week for months, we rehearsed endlessly. I did learn a lot about small theatrical productions, but learned very little additional Spanish. Even with all the rehearsals, it wasn't going very well. With not much promise from his lead male, about a month from opening night my professor decided that I would "no longer attempt to understand the language." That decision was perfectly fine by me, it was already clear in my head that I didn't understand the Spanish language at all. I wasn't sure how anything had changed through his eureka moment.

On opening night I was unbelievably nervous. Not because I was about to perform in front of a large crowd in an intimate theater, but because I was afraid that the audience would realize what I knew already. I knew that throughout the entire seventy minute course of emotionally charged dialogue that the young lady and I would bring to life, I literally had no idea what I was saying.

At one point in the story, I had to profess my love and kiss the beautiful young Latina. But I had no idea what I was actually saying to her. The sweet nothings that I whispered to her in Spanish right before the kiss, were actually nothings to me.

At another point during the performance, I moseyed toward a street lamp on stage. All I knew was that I was supposed to mosey toward the street lamp at that moment. I didn't have a clue as to why I was moseying, or yelling, or frowning, or kneeling, or kissing. I had directions from my professor and my co-star during the final month's rehearsals as to when I should be sad, happy, distraught, and when I was supposed to kiss her. I could act out the expected emotions appropriately, but I had no idea what the words coming out of my mouth meant.

I had memorized one hour and ten minutes of a foreign language script. Every word of it was spoken in fluent Spanish. But it all may as well have been Greek to me. I had no clue what I was talking about.

After the opening performance we received a standing ovation and the beautiful young actress spoke to the audience in fluent Spanish. I could only assume that she was thanking the audience for coming to see us that evening. I just stood there with her on my arm, looking quite dapper in my tuxedo, handsomely sporting a Cheshire grin. I was, however, literally lost in translation.

Members of the audience approached me after the play and started speaking to me in Spanish. "Yo no hablo Español" (I do not speak Spanish), I interrupted politely.

This statement perplexed them so much that I had to insist I was telling the truth. Evidently my "very animated facial features and entertaining responses" had worked. After the audience member's chuckles concerning my evidently unbelievable comment, I had to clarify.

"I really do not speak Spanish," I said in English with a disappointed smirk.

"You have got to be kidding me?" was their reply. First in Spanish, and then realizing I was telling the truth, switching to English.

I had memorized the entire play, word by un-comprehended word. And had regurgitated it with enough believability to strike up casual conversations in a language I did not understand at all.

For my efforts, I received an A+ in Spanish 200 after three performances.

I could accomplish anything Wittenberg threw at me, and anything life threw at me as well. I truly believed that. It was a great time to be alive as Joel A. Capell.

Life was good, or "la vida era buena." I hope that is the correct translation. Thank goodness for Google Translator.

II

Length of War

I REMEMBER exactly where I was and exactly what I was doing on September 11th, 2001. I will always remember, as that day's infamous events changed my life forever. Where were you, Jennifer? I'd like to know. For some reason we have never had that conversation, so I don't know. And I'd like to know everything there is to know about you.

SEPTEMBER 11TH, 2001

During the peak of the American housing market in the early 2000's, the wealthier suburbs of Columbus, Ohio were booming. I was part of a contracting crew that was building new mansions on every corner formerly occupied by corn fields. On that particular morning we were in Granville, Ohio installing the sub-floor on a large home. It was our third new home in the small, eccentric town that summer. I remember it being particularly hot that morning. Our entire crew was working steadily and enjoying the early rays of sunshine. From my eyes, it was another absolutely beautiful day to be alive while wearing my tool belt.

Fourteen years after cutting down the oak tree for a bridge to my boyhood fortress, I was still swinging away and cutting lumber. Currently, I was doing so with a framing hammer and power tools. At the time we were working in Granville, I was about a year out of college and had life by the horns. I was young, newly married, had a well-paying job, and a nice new crew cab pick-up truck. In either my work boots or my combat boots, life was good.

The Army had delivered on its original promise of 60% paid college tuition. And I had just signed my second six year enlistment for the new promise of the Army paying off the student loans that I had incurred. Six more years in the military would essentially provide me with a degree from Wittenberg University, where tuition was well over $26,000 a year when I graduated, at an out of pocket tuition cost of $000.00. I cannot say it was free, because nothing is free. I would have to perform my next six years of enlistment time working diligently in support of our great nation. And that would certainly come at a cost, as did the previous six years. But at the time I was willing to pay those costs.

> Jennifer, having my tuition 100% paid for was well worth the insignificant surprises from the military up to this point in my life. The Army was a great option for me to pay for college prior to September 11th, 2001. It's still a great option to pay for college, but current military requirements have obviously become considerably greater due to the War on Terror. While I certainly do not regret my decision to enlist, when I think about our kids going to college I ponder if I would make that same decision today?

Mid subfloor installation that morning, our boss unapologetically interrupted. He yelled loudly while motioning with his arm for all of us to come over to the yellow DeWalt, contractor grade radio, which we listened to on every jobsite. Immediately noticing the concern on his face, we began to pay attention in awe and disbelief as the news reporters interrupted the normal broadcasting.

The broadcasters were telling us that a passenger jet had flown directly into the side of one of the World Trade Center towers in New York City. Early that morning, we were still unaware of the circumstances surrounding the incident. We didn't yet know if it was a tragic accident or some manner of attack against the United States? Within minutes these reports were the only thing coming across the radio airwaves, on every station and every broadcast. Eager for more information, we loaded up and headed into downtown Granville to find an early lunch and a television.

It was around 10:30 AM, and evidently many others had had the same notion that morning. We couldn't even find a place to park in downtown Granville. There were scores of blue collar workers crowded around the televisions inside every restaurant. Even the necktie and slacks population had managed to escape their offices and scheduled meetings in an attempt to find out what was happening in our homeland. You could hear a pin drop between the timely gasps of astonishment while the reporters tried to explain each newly released video. They were now confirming that it was indeed an act of terrorism.

A group of Middle Eastern men had hijacked several passenger jets in a premeditated and well-orchestrated attack on the United States. The first of these terrorist acts culminated in a terrorist pilot launching himself, his hijacked jet, and all of its passengers into the side of one of the World Trade Center towers. Seeing the actual footage of these horrid acts for the first time was both perplexing and horrifying.

About an hour into our news broadcast viewing, I received a phone call from my Army unit's Readiness NCO (Non-Commissioned Officer) in Norwalk, Ohio. He told me to make sure my bags were packed. All of my military gear, and I, needed to be ready to move at a moment's notice. My unit, Charlie Company 612th Engineer Battalion, along with the entire U.S. Army, was ordered to a high alert status.

As so many Americans did on that day, I went home early to be with my family after hearing the news that our nation was under attack. I left the diner in Granville after eating my early lunch and went home to pack my Army bags to the best of my ability. It was the first time I had packed every single thing into my bags since returning home from Basic Training.

On that day there were four passenger jets that were hijacked, and multiple attacks, which killed thousands of Americans. Both of the World Trade Center towers eventually collapsed after two separate airplanes, one per tower, directly impacted the two towers. And another kamikaze attack successfully reached its target when a third passenger jet crashed into the Pentagon in Washington D.C.

The fourth airplane that was hijacked that morning was United Airlines Flight 93. The potential act of terrorism that had been planned for this flight was thwarted by its passengers. It crashed into a field in Pennsylvania before reaching its intended destination of devastation. It was later claimed by jihadist groups that the original target for Flight 93 was the White House.

The following is an excerpt from an article on United Airlines Flight 93.

After the hijackers took control of the (Flight 93) plane, several passengers and flight attendants learned from phone calls that suicide attacks had already been made by hijacked airliners on the World Trade Center in New York City and the Pentagon in Arlington County, Virginia. Many of the passengers then attempted to regain control of the aircraft from the hijackers. During the struggle, the plane crashed into a field... 130 miles (210 km) northwest of Washington, D.C.

Of the four aircraft hijacked on September 11 – the others were American Airlines Flight 11, United Airlines Flight 175 and American Airlines Flight 77 – United Airlines Flight 93 was the only aircraft that did not reach its hijackers' intended target. Vice President Dick Cheney, in the Presidential Emergency Operations Center deep under the White House, upon learning of the premature crash, is reported to have said, "I think an act of heroism just took place on that plane." (United Airlines Flight 93 n.d.)

President George W. Bush read what would eventually be designated the "Bush Doctrine" to the people of the United States soon after the attacks.

The phrase "Bush Doctrine" described the policy that the United States had the right to secure itself against countries that harbor or give aid to terrorist groups. It was used to describe specific policy elements, including a strategy of "preemptive strikes" as a defense against an immediate or perceived future threat to the security of the United States. This policy principle was applied particularly in the Middle East to counter international terrorist organizations. (Bush Doctrine n.d.)

Some critics have said that the Bush Doctrine was used to validate the declaration of the "Global War on Terrorism" and to occupy various countries across the Middle East. I would in turn say that they are partially correct with that statement. The Bush Doctrine was used, but it did not validate anything. A jihadist group had just punched us in the face! The mere words of our President were not needed for validation. My opinion will forever stand firm that the U.S. would never establish better validation to occupy the Middle East than the invitation received on 9/11.

At the time I had no idea of the impact that those acts of terrorism would have on my life. I don't believe anyone understood the impact that they would have on America, or on the rest of the world.

Since September 11th, 2001, remembered today as 9/11, my bags have never been unpacked.

THE ARMY VALUES

LOYALTY, DUTY, RESPECT, SELFLESS SERVICE, HONOR, INTEGRITY, PERSONAL COURAGE

A country united, indeed the United States was obligated to do something in reaction to the 9/11/2001 attacks on our own soil. However, I am certain that not a single person making decisions on 9/12/2001 thought we would still be fighting that battle sixteen years later.

These next few stories jump ahead quite a few years to 2017-2018. They are placed right after the 9/11 story and relatively early in these memoirs to illustrate just how long I, and many of my fellow brothers and sisters in arms, have been fighting the seemingly endless War on Terror.

ROUND 17

For nearly the entire 2017 calendar year and into early 2018, I have been deployed to the Middle East. It is quite disheartening being overseas on yet another deployment and realizing that there is still no visible end to this conflict. The United States military and our allies have been fighting the War on Terror for sixteen long years, and just the tiniest speck of light at the end of the tunnel is still unseen.

As a soldier who has been in the Army since the inception of the war, I am tired. A deployment or preparing for a looming deployment has been part of my life for nearly half of my forty trips around the sun.

In the following excerpts from a Congressional Research Service report titled "The Islamic State and U.S. Policy", dated February of 2017, Middle Eastern affairs specialist Christopher M. Blanchard and Middle Eastern affairs analyst Carla E. Humud write about former President Obama's policy for defeating ISIS, and the transfer of this authority to President Trump.

The Obama Administration led a multilateral coalition in support of its stated goal to "degrade and ultimately destroy" the Islamic State (IS)... The Administration's strategy to achieve this objective consisted of a number of "lines of effort," including, in partnership with several European and Arab states: direct military action, support for Iraqi and Syrian partner ground forces, intelligence gathering and sharing, and efforts to restrict flows of foreign fighters, disrupt the Islamic State's finances, and eliminate its leaders.

President Obama's stated goals for U.S. strategy were to "degrade and ultimately defeat" the Islamic State through "direct military action and support for local partner forces". Administration officials expressed increasing confidence in the implementation of U.S. and allied military strategy in Iraq and Syria.

President Donald Trump and leading national security officials in his Administration have articulated their desire to "destroy the Islamic State" organization, with the White House saying in its overarching description of the President's foreign policy approach that "defeating ISIS and other radical Islamic terror groups will be our highest priority." (Blanchard and Humud, 2017)

Round after excruciating round we have continued to enter the ring in this official boxing match with terrorist idealisms. Three different U.S. Presidents have led sixteen rounds and counting, if we count one round per year. The calendar year has just flipped to 2018, and I'm not certain that any of us know who we are supposed to swing at anymore. Ding, ding... round seventeen.

Within these pages, I cannot fathom making a dent in the complex situation that is the Middle East. "Radio Silence" is certainly not intended to be a history lesson. However, on a recommendation from a well-respected colleague, "a broad operational picture" is included here. The inclusion has been an incredible addition to the narrative as a whole. The research required to deliver the big picture accurately has definitely provided me a deeper understanding of the region and its volatile nature. This has been an unforeseen bonus.

The information contained in the next several paragraphs is a combination of my own knowledge, various references cited within "Radio Silence", and current events. Without further ado, here is the extremely abbreviated and mostly paraphrased Joel Capell explanation of some pertinent facts on the Middle East since 9/11.

Less than one month after 9/11/2001, then President George W. Bush authorized the first airstrikes on jihadist groups located in Afghanistan. Since the first airstrike, the U.S. Global War on Terrorism efforts in Afghanistan have been supported by over 40 countries from across the globe. The United Nations (UN) formed the International Security Assistance Force (ISAF) as the authority over those 40+ countries. Since its formation, ISAF has assisted the Afghani government with current operational needs.

In 2003, Operation Iraqi Freedom and "democratic change" for Iraq kicked off against the Ba'athist party regime and Saddam Hussein. Al-Qaeda surfaced quickly into the "void of power" in Iraq after Saddam was captured and later executed. Iraq held its first democratic election in 2005 and published a constitution, but Sunni and Shiite Muslim's religious differences meant the country would remain divided internally.

Separate from Al-Qaeda, a new growing jihadist group in Iraq, built and led by Abu Musab al Zarqawi, purposefully took advantage of Sunni Muslim animosity. Sunnis felt left out of the new Shia Muslim led "democracy" that the U.S. had forged in Iraq. Under al Zarqawi's leadership, they formed the Islamic State of Iraq (ISI). Zarqawi was killed in an airstrike by U.S. forces in June of 2006. One year later, the ISI reorganized and renamed itself the Islamic State of Iraq and the Levant. ISIL/ISIS was officially born.

In an attempt to reestablish the caliphate (religious leadership succession), ISIS appointed its own authority, or "caliph", in religious succession to the Prophet Mohammed. According to ISIS, he would have authority over all the world's Muslims. All those who reject the new caliph's authority are considered infidels and are given three choices: convert to Islam, pay a "protection tax", or death.

Despite the fact that Muslims have been charging infidels, Christians and especially Jews, protection taxes for centuries, the reestablishment of the caliphate by ISIS has turned out to be a grave mistake. By doing so, they have alienated themselves from many Islamic leaders who question ISIS' authority to nominate a supreme leader for all of Islam.

> Jennifer, I personally find it disturbing that some Islamic leaders do not question ISIS' three choices for infidels, but rather only their authority to nominate a supreme leader.

ISIS evolved as a result of unforeseen instability in the Middle East due to religious differences between Sunni and Shia Muslims, a "void of power" created by the U.S. overthrow of the Ba'athist party, and the eventual U.S. withdraw from the region. ISIS has since then changed its name to the Islamic State (IS) in order to present a worldwide united front.

> Jennifer, within "Radio Silence" I will thoroughly reject ISIS' request to be formally recognized as the unified Islamic State or IS. As most of my military brethren do, I will continue to refer to the jihadist group as ISIS. In our eyes these group(s), regardless of their name, have already been afforded their last reorganization effort.

After ousting Saddam Hussein, the U.S. led coalition fought to keep the Iraqi people free from influential jihadist groups as well as free from their own internal differences, until the U.S. "officially" withdrew from Iraq at the end of 2011.

Meanwhile in Afghanistan, the Taliban remained active throughout the nine years of U.S. occupation in Iraq. International Security Assistance Force (ISAF) counterinsurgency operations were stepped up in Afghanistan as Taliban guerilla warfare and suicide attacks escalated through 2009. In 2011 ISAF troop numbers, mostly American soldiers, peaked. Afterwards, the withdrawal from Afghanistan by U.S. forces was the intent of our leaders, as the Taliban seemed to retreat into thin air.

Throughout this time, coalition forces continued their search for key jihadist leaders worldwide. And in 2011, a U.S. Navy Seal team raided a compound in Pakistan where they killed Osama Bin Laden. Bin Laden was considered to be the father of Al-Qaeda, and the mastermind behind the September 11, 2001 attacks on the U.S.

In 2014, then President Barack Obama ended the official combat mission in Afghanistan, Operation Enduring Freedom. Security of the Afghani people was officially transferred to the continually corrupt Afghan government. Although the official operation is over, several thousand U.S. and allied troops continue their support in Afghanistan, and are expected to remain there through the foreseeable future.

In early 2013 in Iraq, roughly two years after the 2011 official U.S. withdrawal, ISIS had once again grown into a powerful force. They had also amassed a large foothold in the neighboring country of Syria. From mid-2013 through present day the build-up of coalition forces and assistance to local national government forces in both Iraq and Syria have effectively pushed the ISIS stronghold back, but their influences remain strong.

As of January 1st, 2018, many smaller, but nonetheless important, known jihadist rebel or revolutionary groups of U.S. interest are currently found operating openly in the countries of Iraq, Iran, Syria, Pakistan, Egypt, Yemen, Libya, Sudan, Somalia and Nigeria.

In Afghanistan, on January 27th, 2018, the Taliban publically claimed a suicide bombing that utilized an ambulance to enter a hospital. The attack killed 95 civilians.

Turkey, which neighbors both Iraq and Syria to the north, has just bombed a city populated by Kurdish citizens located on the Syrian-Turkish border.

And here we are… February, 2018. In less than 30 days I will be home from my current deployment.

I'll conclude this brief overview with a statement. "This war will never end."

As a veteran who embraces the suck of this discouraging and endless war, I'll inject some dark humor and propose a few sarcastic questions to ponder.

Like a shady small business might do in order to evade bankruptcy, do terrorist groups merely shut down, move across the street, and open back up under a new name? Al-Qaeda, Taliban, ISI, ISIL, ISIS… who's next? As the ensuing excerpt indicates, will the next named batter simply step up to the plate?

> *Secretary of State Rex Tillerson said that defeating the Islamic State globally may be "extremely challenging" and said that depriving the group of its so-called caliphate in the Middle East "will not defeat ISIS once and for all, it will simply morph into its next version."* (Blanchard and Humud, 2017)

The Iraqi city of Mosul has been "liberated" multiple times over the last seventeen years. Mosul's most recent liberation occurred in late 2017. Shortly after that liberation, U.S. President Donald Trump and Russian President Vladimir Putin shook hands and declared victory over ISIS in Syria.

Regardless, I still didn't get to go home after that "victory" was declared. In fact I am still in the Middle East and we are still "fighting ISIS", months after that victory was declared. We have been victorious many times, but in each of these instances victory has not been a precursor to the end.

Do we have a realistic chance of reforming a culture that predates American colonialism by a couple thousand years? Will we ever be able to entirely defeat ISIS, or the next jihadist group, under its new name? We have been attempting to do so for seventeen years and there is still no light at the end of this never ending dark tunnel.

Actually winning the Global War on Terrorism, or reaching the point of "game over, thanks for playing, you can go home now", is a most daunting task that a large portion of the world has undertaken. Up to this point, victories have been won, but the war has not.

To date, the Islamic State (IS) organization and its regional adherents have thrived in ungoverned or under-governed areas of countries affected by conflict or political instability. These permissive environments provide resources and safe-haven for IS operations and in some cases offer recruits from among disaffected local groups. The prospects and options for undermining IS supporters have been shaped by the relative success or failure of efforts to restore security, address political grievances, boost economic growth, and promote effective governance.

Military operations may eliminate IS fighters and liberate IS-held territory, but underlying political disputes and development challenges that have been exploited by the Islamic State and other extremist groups may remain unaddressed or become amplified if post- conflict reconciliation and reconstruction needs go unmet. (Blanchard and Humud, 2017)

No matter the actual length of a war in years, most Soldiers who have found themselves in combat will state that war lasts a lifetime. In 2018, seventeen years after 9/11/2001, I am currently deployed again, and I am tired. For more than just a few of those seventeen years of my life, I have literally been on the run.

JEN, MAYBE you will find them less risky than I do, but I must admit that it has been difficult to wrap my head around a few of the tactics we have used during this deployment.

NEW HOPE & TACTICS

Throughout my 2017-2018 deployment, I have been involved logistically in what was originally the Obama Administration's "line of effort" toward "support for Iraqi and Syrian partner ground forces". A multination task force of Americans, British, Australians, Swedes, Finnish, Singaporeans, and Canadians, has been working together in Kuwait to supply a militia of "local partner forces" with the means to fight ISIS. The supplies are provided mostly at the expense of the U.S. taxpayer, under a congressionally approved decree called the Counter-ISIS Train and Equip Fund, or CTEF. The supplies are routed through Kuwait as their last stopping point before being given to the local partner forces.

Here's a short excerpt on Kuwait and its continued partnership with the coalition.

Kuwait joined the U.S.-led coalition against the Islamic State along with the other Gulf Cooperation Council states in September 2014. Its most significant participation has been hosting the operational headquarters for Operation Inherent Resolve (OIR). "ARCENT"—the U.S. Army component of U.S. Central Command is based in Kuwait, and the ARCENT commander serves as overall U.S. commander of OIR. Kuwait has provided over $9 billion in humanitarian support in Syria, Iraq, Jordan, and Lebanon to assist civilians and help regional governments cope with refugee flows from these conflicts. That amount makes Kuwait the second largest single country donor to these efforts, led only by the United States. Kuwait also hosts about 145,000 Syrian citizens who fled the war there. (Katzman, 2017)

Among the factions of the local partner forces whom CTEF supplies, are the actual Iraqi and Syrian nation's armies, some non-recognized tribes and militant groups, and a few small mercenary forces only loyal to themselves. All of these local partner forces have been vetted by the U.S. as responsible parties to fight ISIS in northern Iraq and Syria. An opposition to ISIS and a willingness to fight are the only qualifying or vetting factors that I can perceive.

CTEF is a bit of a rogue operation because the mission we undertake does not function according to any written military doctrine. We operate in conjunction with a Special Operations Joint Task Force that has multiple members embedded within the Syrian and Iraqi local partner forces. Supplies are distributed according to the recommendations of the embedded Special Operations soldiers. Any type of involvement with Special Ops is typically under the radar, making the initial idea of being in direct support of the "tip of the spear" exciting to those of us on the CTEF mission.

Over time, a few opinions, including my own, regarding the CTEF mission's practices and so-called progress have changed considerably. One drastic conclusion may refer to the development of CTEF as an unusual form of slavery, being opportunistically utilized for the benefit of the so-called western cause. CTEF's success no doubt lies in part to the vast oppression among the people of the Middle East.

The CTEF program creates something of an "anti-ISIS" gang mentality. It does so by providing the people of these deprived areas with a lifestyle and prestige. Since we don't want ISIS to recruit the people of these nations, we do our own recruiting. Their local and national governments receive war winning equipment in exchange for armies who fight on our side, rather than with ISIS.

Even though this war against ISIS is quite possibly "their war" more than it is ours, I personally do not care for the thought that we are in a way, inhumanely "buying" mercenaries to fight it.

Another point of contention to the CTEF program is that we are simply handing over billions of dollars of arms, ammunition, vehicles, and war winning power to these local forces. We have no real assurance that they will be fighting on our side tomorrow.

However, one of the benefits to the CTEF program is that we do allow the ownership of the fight to rest on the shoulders of the people that ISIS is recruiting. In turn, coalition forces are providing leadership and direction, but are not doing the majority of the actual fighting. Americans and our allies are not being Killed In Action (KIA) in the current efforts to nullify ISIS. War torn Iraq and Syria lack the money and supplies to effectively rid their homeland of the radical jihadist group, so their forces take up our supplied armaments, funneled through CTEF, and are for the most part doing the fighting on the ground.

There is no doubt about the evil that ISIS represents, even among citizens within the Middle East. The people of these nations are willing to fight against ISIS, and they are winning.

> *It (Islamic State, IS) has lost large amounts of territory since mid-2015, and its remaining territories have become increasingly isolated from each other in the face of ongoing and planned operations by the U.S.-led international military coalition and a number of U.S.-backed local forces. Having (IS has) ceded approximately 60% of the populated territory it once held in Iraq, and approximately 30% of the populated territory it once held in Syria. U.S. officials estimate that tens of thousands of IS fighters have died in battle, with their numbers (having been) reduced to an estimated force strength of 12,000 to 15,000 fighters in Iraq and Syria. U.S. officials also state that morale among IS fighters has worsened and that the group's finances, recruitment streams, communications, public outreach, and leadership have been substantially disrupted.* (Blanchard and Humud, 2017)

The soldiers performing the CTEF mission spend countless hours tracking all the arms and war winning equipment that we distribute to our local partner forces. Properly recording and tracking the supplies we distribute is lawfully part of the congressionally approved CTEF mission. So many questions about "the CTEF law" and how to properly track all the distributions have arisen, that the Department of Military Logistics has become involved in the tracking process.

The Department of Military Logistics is the organization responsible for planning and carrying out the movement of supplies during a war. Logistics are absolutely crucial in deciding the outcome of a war.

Nearly everyone understands the need for the military to be auditable. Nobody understands that better than The Department of Military Logistics. Four of their top level executives from Washington D.C. were sent on an auditing field trip to Kuwait, so they could better understand the tracking process which CTEF utilizes, and possibly help us improve it.

CTEF is required to track every single bullet from purchase to local forces delivery, so we were fairly certain we could provide The Department of Military Logistics with all of the required and requested auditable information. And with a few quick calculations from our very simple spreadsheet tracking process, we did provide that information to them.

A few weeks after their auditing field trip ended, the Department's "recommendations for improvement" mandated that we utilize their contracted tracking system. A contracted system is one which is utilized according to an ongoing government contract. Typically, an ongoing government contract is written to receive funding according to utilization numbers. So, by mandating CTEF to be a new user to their tracking system, the Department of Military Logistics would receive additional funding from the Army.

Their system, however, never fit into how the unconventional CTEF mission operates. Regardless of that fact we have spent 4-5 months adapting our practices to attempt to fit their contracted system.

At ground level, the process has gone just about how I expected it would. Converting to the new system has improved nothing. In fact, it has made a mess of the tracking process. But what do I know? I am only a twenty plus year veteran, with eleven years of experience in military logistics systems. I'd like to think that there are a few good reasons why we converted to the contracted system, but not a single benefit can be seen by the likes of us in CTEF.

An inability to access and/or see the bigger picture is an endless frustration for military personnel worldwide. Like the individual parts of any bureaucracy, we individual military sections struggle to maintain motivation, while rarely seeing the big picture or the fruits of our labors. The military rightfully recognizes and seeks improvements in its processes in order to avoid becoming stagnant. But there are certainly instances when, "because that's the way we've always done it" suffices.

Soldiers want to know why? I understand the timely need to follow orders. But in most instances, those of us behind the front lines should be afforded that information, if for no other reason than to maintain our own morale.

Most of us see the inherent CTEF tracking problem being that once the war winning equipment leaves our hands, and it is given to the local forces, we no longer have any method to track it. Billions of dollars of weapons and war winning equipment has been distributed, and for purposes of U.S. military tracking, is lost into the thin air of the Middle Eastern countryside. We know who we have given it to, but actually finding it all again, if that ever becomes a directive, will be a nightmare that I am glad I will not be around to undertake. The Dept. of Military Logistics never gave a second thought to this disappearing act.

What the hell does it matter what system we utilize to track the equipment? I will forever fail to see the logic in the amount of time and money spent in order to convert to the expensive tracking system. Which certainly does not work any better for our CTEF mission.

In my opinion, however, there is an illogical reason why we converted to the Department's tracking system. That reason is contracts. And contracts make money. There is plenty of money, and tracking CTEF equipment through a contracted logistics system is another way for someone to make it. For our mission, Microsoft Excel and emails have proven to work just fine.

What is a soldier to do? Fight against Washington D.C.? Raise a ruckus to my bosses, ranks above me, that they are wrong in this instance? Converting to the contracted tracking system isn't that big of a deal right? I don't have enough rank to make that decision, evidently none of us do. Washington D.C. must know something that we don't. As U.S. citizens and as soldiers, we just want to know why!

Drive on soldier. We all value our careers, so like the countless numbers before us, we refrain from communicating our discontent, and maintain radio silence.

If the equipment we gave away cannot be tracked after the point of delivery, the natural question is: what will happen to all the weapons and well supplied armies after the war?

If there ever is an actual end to this war, will the forces we are supplying simply go back to their age old wars of fighting each other? The possibility also exists for the various local partner forces to unify and utilize the weapons we are supplying to them against us, years down the road.

Is CTEF similar to "Charlie Wilson's War"? The true story of "Charlie Wilson's War" (George Crile III, published in 2003), is about the U.S. supplying weapons to Afghanistan so Afghans could ward off the Russian invasion in the early 1980's. In Afghanistan, in 1979, the Mujahedeen was originally born to expel the Russian invasion of Afghanistan. A faction of the Mujahedeen eventually became the Taliban. Supplying weapons to Afghanistan in the early 1980's ended up biting the U.S. in the ass during their own Taliban conflicts in Afghanistan, years later. It was confirmed more than once that the Taliban were indeed using weapons against coalition forces that the United States had supplied to Afghanistan 25 years prior.

Will CTEF's distributions end up biting us in the ass?

The CTEF mission is an odd undertaking and somewhat of a gamble, with global implications. Regardless of the humanity of the mission, or the risks taken, the facts are that CTEF provides local forces with materials to defeat ISIS, and those tactics are working. And in the current scheme of things, that's what really matters.

IS IT POSSIBLE that the CTEF mission is actually supplying a Middle Eastern civil war? Are we effectively arming these armies and mercenary warrior groups in order for them to take each other out in a facilitated and accelerated war on their own homeland battleground?

Because of my own humanity, I truly do not believe that coalition forces "hope", or "intend" for a civil war to occur. But through no fault of our own, the world has now witnessed a short lived civil war in Iraq. And internally, members of CTEF have witnessed several altercations between the "good guy" local partner forces factions. All of these forces are struggling for power in Iraq and Syria.

OLD HATRED

I stated in the previous story that the CTEF mission is an odd undertaking and somewhat of a gamble, with global implications. A few examples of the gamble that we are taking can be seen coming to fruition clearly through the short stories that follow. But first, an introduction of the Kurdish people of northern Iraq is an order.

America has been silently allied with the Kurdistan Regional Government (KRG) of Iraq since 1988, when Saddam Hussein killed thousands of Kurdish people in northern Iraq with chemical warfare. The Kurdish people have since operated in opposition to Bagdad and the Iraqi state. They rejoiced in the streets when allied forces captured Saddam fifteen years later, in 2003.

A significant point of contention with the KRG remains the KRG's marketing of crude oil exports separately from Baghdad.
(Katzman and Humud, 2016)

The KRG desire a free nation to call their own. They already have their own military in the Kurdish Peshmerga, fly their own flag, and pay their own taxes. They believe that land in parts of Turkey, Syria, and Iran, as well as northern Iraq, should be included as part of their liberated nation.

In late 2017, the Kurdish people held a Kurdish Referendum, in which they voted for their freedom. It passed by a large majority. They began to wage their own war on the Iraqi state in an attempt to claim the oil rich region of Kirkuk, which is populated mostly by Kurdish people in northern Iraq. But their attempts to claim what they believe to be their entitled lands were immediately thwarted by the Iraqi army.

Both the Iraqi army and the Kurdish Peshmerga are "local partner forces" being supplied by CTEF. The "civil war" I mentioned earlier, did briefly come to fruition. But after about a week of televised skirmishes, the results of the short internal conflict left the borders of Kurdistan yet to be officially drawn.

Now I have introduced the four main factions (there are many additional smaller ones) that have during recent history been in contention for power in Iraq, and now also in Syria. The first, Sunni Muslims, and the second, Shiite Muslims, have been unable come to an agreement due to religious differences. The third faction, to whom any name for a jihadist group may be given, will not come to a civilized agreement with anyone, period. And the fourth, the Kurdish people, who would like to be permanently independent from the four different countries in which they reside. They want to form their own nation right in the center of it all.

But wait! There's more! For a limited time only… at the arbitrary cost of billions of dollars… in addition to this already explosive deal of a lifetime… a free dosage of testosterone like none other!

Adding to this already volatile situation, the United States is currently giving three of these parties' free weapons (to fight ISIS of course) through CTEF.

What, we have here is… a failure… to communicate.

In short, the situation is an extremely unstable, political and military mess. These four different groups of people, with ethnic, religious, and national differences, have been fighting with each other while coexisting for thousands of years. A natural conclusion would be that these people may desire to finally put aside their differences in order to refrain from continuous war. Not in the Middle East! Specifically in both Iraq and Syria, old hatred currently reigns.

Unfortunately, public versions of hatred can still be found in America, and Americans still have some much needed work to do. Thankfully though, we have come an extremely long way. The majority of Americans don't know what relentless, day in and day out hatred looks like. The same held true for me, until I witnessed the Middle East. Hatred in America does not even come close to what can be seen on a daily basis within the Middle East.

In a seemingly hopeless situation of endless hatred, I'll once again inject some sarcastic humor. It's what veteran's do.

The Middle East reminds me of the old Looney Tunes cartoon with the sheepdog and the coyote, Sam and Ralph, respectively.

Each morning Sam and Ralph show up for work, clock-in for the day while exchanging pleasantries, and share a cup of tea together. They manage to put all their differences aside… for the moment.

Then the whistle blows, and it's time to go to work.

Sam's job is to protect the sheep in the flock. Ralph's job is to try to eat the sheep. So the two proceed to fight with each other throughout the entire morning.

Then the whistle blows, and it's time for lunch.

During lunch, Sam and Ralph sit on a hillside together, underneath the shade tree, while eating cookies and talking about baseball. They do so as if the last four hours of attempted homicide never happened.

Wickedly, seconds before the whistle announces to the two characters that lunch is over, Ralph sneaks away so he can get a head start on capturing a sheep for his dinner.

The whistle blows and lunch is over.

All afternoon Ralph literally attempts to kill Sam in various catastrophic Looney Tunes ways, so he can capture a sheep from the flock. But, somehow Sam is always the wiser to Ralphs plans.

Then the whistle blows, and the work day is over.

Sam and Ralph once again exchange pleasantries, clock-out for the day, and forecast returning to work tomorrow for much of the same debauchery.

"Good night Ralph," from Sam. "Good night Sam," from Ralph.

Like Sam and Ralph, Middle Easterners are fully capable of cohabitating, but they have some enormous differences that they are willing to die for. When it's time for them to conduct business, those differences are all placed directly on the table. But, behind closed doors or after work hours, it is okay to break bread and have tea with yesterday's enemies.

Here are a couple specific Middle Eastern examples about how Sam and Ralph hate each other, even though they coexist as neighbors.

In late 2017, about the same timeframe as the Kurdish Referendum vote, the CTEF team had prepared ten older model U.S. military hummers to be "divested" to the Kurdish Peshmerga fighters allied with the KRG. In layman terms we were giving the Peshmerga hummers to fight ISIS. Keep in mind that the U.S. was providing both the Iraqi Army and the Peshmerga forces (among others) with the same types of equipment in support of the war against ISIS, through the CTEF program. We were organizing deliveries like this one almost daily, to these vetted groups so they could fight ISIS across northern Iraq and Syria.

Somewhere in northern Iraq, the civilian run transportation convoy that was delivering these ten hummers to the Peshmerga had been stopped at a standard security checkpoint. The checkpoint was meant to ensure the convoy's legal right to transport the previously mentioned ten U.S.

owned military hummers. The convoy was stopped and the correct documents were presented.

Simultaneously, the progress of an Iraqi Army faction led by an identified and vetted Iraqi Army Colonel was halted at the same checkpoint. He and his subordinates were also fighting ISIS. The weapons they were carrying and the vehicles that they were in were all supplied by CTEF. Essentially, the entire mass of vehicles at the checkpoint were all part of the same team, fighting ISIS.

The Iraqi Colonel asked one of the security checkpoint guards where the hummers on the transport convoy were headed. The hummer's final destination, the Kurdish Peshmerga forces, was relayed to the Colonel and he and his faction were allowed to pass the convoy transporting the hummers.

On his way around the convoy, the Iraqi Colonel began yelling viciously and opened fire with his AK-47 on the empty hummers. In doing so he flattened several tires and caused irreversible damage to three of the ten.

The ageless hatred between the Arab and Kurdish peoples had manifested itself through coalition supplied armaments of war.

The animosity between Arab and Kurd is so deeply engrained that it trumps all U.S. attempts toward unification. Coalition leadership understands the fight against ISIS as the unifying factor between them all, but the people of these Middle Eastern regions only understand their hatred for each other.

I'll finish this letter entitled "Old Hatred", with one additional example of an age old hatred that reigns far above all others aforementioned in the Middle East. That hatred is between the Jews and the Muslims, or between Israel and nearly everyone else.

The Israelis are indirectly involved in the CTEF mission. They, among other countries, donate humanitarian and medical supplies for coalition forces to divest to the local partner forces. Among the supplies donated were thousands of sterile bandages that happened to have Hebrew writing on the packaging. Knowing that this may seem offensive to Muslims, CTEF personnel "cleaned" the bandages by removing all the packaging that contained any reference to Judaism or Israel.

When American CTEF soldiers attempted to give the bandages to the Muslim local partner forces, to be used on their wounded, the American soldiers were told that the bandages would be set on fire if they were left in the vicinity. Somehow, the local partner forces were aware that the bandages were from Israel. These Muslims would rather watch those Israeli donated bandages burn, than place one of them on one of their own bleeding and dying men.

The unfading hatred between Muslim and Jew had manifested itself through coalition supplied humanitarian medical aid. It is an ageless hatred which Westerners do not have the current power to influence.

Maybe within my lifetime I will get to see peace in the Middle East. Maybe not…

III

Stuff of Legend

THESE NEXT few letters are about experiences that have assisted in the shaping of my opinions. They will play a part in the entirety of this story. Jen, I'd like you to understand these things before we meet my skeletons.

This particular story takes a look at some of the issues the military faces along with my perception of changes within military culture over my years of service. The title of this short story refers to a military force of men and women ("women" should be included with the word "men" accordingly, in future references) during a much less stressful, seemingly mythical time for our nation before 9/11/2001. As you know Jennifer, war can be very stressful for both a soldier and their family members before, during, and many years afterwards.

OF MYTHS AND MEN

Prior to 9/11/2001, military training consisted of men and women performing their actual Army job. The training consisted of long days, was tough, sweaty, and dirty. Let's take a look an Army mechanic for instance. From dawn until dusk a mechanic would essentially fix Army vehicles. For a couple hours after fixing vehicles they'd tell stories, drink beer, play cards and laugh a lot about the mishaps of the day or a friend's small misfortune. And then they went to bed. The next day, rinse and repeat. Overall, not much has changed over time with these themes.

But the stakes were elevated after 9/11/2001, when the War on Terror created a stronghold on our nation. Instead of focusing on how to win this War, we began to allow distracting and self-degrading principals to invade our military forces. Allow me to explain.

Now-a-days a lot of military equipment has become so specialized that the average mechanic is out of touch with the technology. Specific contractors and contracts from outside the military are needed in order service and repair it. The U.S. spends billions of dollars on necessary equipment upgrades for its military, but the military cannot maintain all that equipment anymore without the assistance of contractors. Just like in the civilian automobile market, the manufacturers of military vehicles have imposed years of required maintenance, which makes money for their contracted mechanics. With political lobbying at its worst, our military decision makers have allowed these contractors to essentially drive that money making train. There are now twice as many contractors on most overseas military bases as there are soldiers. Contractors are just behind the front lines of the battlefield, even sometimes on the battlefield, making billions of U.S. taxpayer dollars.

A second example is the reliance on outside contractors to provide meals for soldiers. The Army rarely even cooks its own food anymore. From highly specialized needs all the way down to basic survival, we rely heavily on contractors to do jobs that not too long ago belonged to soldiers.

If it was broken, we used to be the ones who fixed it. If we were hungry, we cooked it. If it needed a button, we sewed it back on. Those types of things made men useful, and feel useful. Men were proud of their daily accomplishments. Hard work and the ability to survive without external influences are two of the founding principles that have made America and its military forces highly successful. These principles also provided something for each of us to be proud of. We could stand together behind these types of accomplishments.

However, we are presently allowing the contractor to steer the War on Terror and they are heading in the opposite direction of those founding principles. Don't take this the wrong way. I believe for the most part these contractors do a good job serving our fighting forces. But the men behind the contracts have a single purpose that presides over all others. That purpose is to make money, heaping piles of money. This form of simple greed certainly does not make our military forces more effective.

Since the inception of contract run sustainment operations, the U.S. military has been overrun with new "required" training. Some of this training consists of viewing PowerPoint briefings on Judge Advocate General (JAG) Hearings, and Proper Fire Extinguisher Usage. Those things do have their proper place, but what soldiers consider important is survivability and winning a war. We just want to go home, alive.

Instead of training on how to win the War on Terror, the U.S. Army's training focus seems to be on our yin properly aligning with our yang. Mandated training on these ideals solidifies the question that most of us ponder. How in the hell does an Army, focusing on things such as these, manifest a military victory? Answer... it doesn't.

Regardless, in 2017, the Army mandated Transgender Awareness Training. We have been forced to learn about individuals who desire to surgically change their birth gender. As American soldiers, persons who have volunteered to enlist in the United States Army and fight for their country, we now know all of the progression points of advancement for a person going through a complete sex change. Meanwhile, soldiers can no longer start a campfire, navigate cross country with a map and a compass, or change a tire on their equipment. Let that sink in for a minute.

Truthfully, I don't personally care what an individual's "gender choice" happens to be. 99% of military personnel would agree with that statement, while adding only one caveat. As long as individuals can perform their required job, we simply do not care. It's not the subject of gender choice that bothers us. It's the situation in which we are taught the subject(s). Learning about Transgenderism doesn't win wars. And most of us really just want to win the war so we can go home!

Jen, this is my favorite deployment quote. It can be found posted on office bulletin boards and on soldier's lockers in deployment sites around the world.

People who challenge me with "go big or go home" seriously underestimate my willingness to go home. It's literally my only goal.

-Unknown

On February 21st, 1995, I raised my right hand and swore to defend our great country in the U.S. Army. And I am proud to fight so my countrymen can be afforded specific freedoms, even if I do not totally agree with them. Who in the hell comes up with this shit for Army training, and why were they ever allowed to make decisions for the military at all? If a person wants to change their birth gender, more power to them. But why do the actions of a few need to be relentlessly shoved down the throats of soldiers through forced acceptance? It's as if the military is some sociological or psychological petri dish for American society.

How in the hell does this help us win the war? Stop stealing our edge, America. Quit forcing your agenda down our throats. Leave us be, and let us be proud.

Years ago, I learned how to "Army" from useful men, who taught me useful things. During my first seven years in the Army, part of our annual training requirements included going to a prison and getting into fights with prison guards… on purpose. The guards taught us some great hand to hand combat skills as part of Riot Reaction Training. We put on face shields, carried large plastic body shields and wielded batons. We attempted to contain the prison guards while they acted like rioting prisoners.

During the first couple scenarios the guards would beat the crap out of us, and all of them would "escape" from prison. We soldiers always "lost the battle" at first. But we listened, we learned, we trained harder, ran through more scenarios, and eventually we stepped up our game. It was violent, it was extreme, and it was bruising and sometimes bloody. It was great training and it was a great amount of fun to be a man, a man of both strength and intellect.

In the required Army training of today, I have received Riot Reaction Training via PowerPoint presentation. While viewing a projector screen and sitting in folding chairs, I partook in Army training with still photos of how to properly hold a riot baton, perform several strikes with said baton, and get into a few protective defense postures.

Evidently, absurdity is now the accepted training norm. Does viewing a PowerPoint presentation effectively teach our next generation of soldier's hand to hand combat skills or how to react to a riot? Hell no!

I had to walk out of the room before I performed several baton-like strikes on the projector.

If the military loses its attitude it becomes ineffective. Does the U.S. want a Rottweiler protecting us from bad guys, or do we want a Labrador retriever? That's what it really boils down to. I firmly believe that the best first defense against evil minded men is through education and stabilization. But if those two societal avenues fail collectively, the best defense against evil men becomes good men who are skilled at violence. That's where the military steps up to the plate. While we are up to bat, if we strike out, we are supposed to rush the pitcher's mound. That's our job! We embrace the suck so America doesn't have too! If America kills off the military's edge, and does not allow the good guys to hone our skills of violence, good luck holding the bad guys at bay.

Jihad is growing in our own back yard. The Labradors bark once and then welcome Jihadists indoors for tea and crumpets. When these terrorists rear their arms and show their snarling teeth, who's going to show up to the fight? Pick your dodge ball team, America. Do we want that team to have the edge or not? Unfortunately, what we are talking about here is not a game. It is very real, it is highly unfair, and it is not something to be messed with.

When our countrymen are cowering in the corner and Johnny Jihad is about to slit throats, I'll ask the question again. Edge or no edge? America, you should leave the guys with the edge alone. We do things that most of you don't want to do. Rottweilers protect the junkyard at all costs. During the dodgeball game we aim and hit right in the face with the rubber ball. And we will do it again while our enemies are spitting blood on the floor. Don't take that edge away from us.

The military needs Rottweilers, not Labrador retrievers. Rottweilers discriminate equally against everyone and will take off a leg if need be. Soldiers are much the same. We are permanently on offense, while in defense of our country.

In the military there is no place for hurt feelings. A Rottweiler doesn't care much about feelings either. Does that make the Rottweiler a bad dog? It depends on the purpose the dog has.

The purpose of our military is to win wars while providing protection for our country. Period! Soldiers are built to neutralize threats, and we need Rottweilers to do this. We need military men and women with the edge. Men do not maintain the edge by watching PowerPoint briefings. Men maintain the edge by practicing it, by getting in fights with prison guards, and by getting in fist fights with each other.

America should not attempt to change the attitude of the military. The military's job is not stability, education and acceptance. War is not stable. A soldier cannot pull the trigger when their own psychology questions their enemy's motive. Soldiers in battle cannot submit because they don't like something, or if something is offensive to them. They most certainly cannot take a knee, or post about how life is so unfair on social media.

Constantly bombarded with "unfairness" over and over again from all avenues, this generation of Americans is actually beginning to believe their lives are unfair. I've got news for them and all those touting this idea. Like my Mother and Father told me, "life is not fair". Utopian society does not exist.

Being unfair mandates a comparison. Unfair compared to what? Americans should take a look at the world around them before stating their own lives are unfair. Spend a month in one of the less fortunate countries of the Middle East or elsewhere around the world, and then talk to me about how "oppressed" or unfortunate we are in America. The whiney and unjustifiable idea that America is somehow unfair is destroying us from the inside out.

On the flip side, some of the greatest social advancements of our time are the direct results of believing things could be better. And I completely understand the need for continued improvement within our social structures. An example of this would be the desegregation of the Armed Forces by President Truman after WWII. Social equality, and advancements in freedom itself, stemmed directly from that action.

Truman, who is considered to have been a great American politician, put that policy in place. Policy implementation is what politicians are supposed to do! Politicians are for stabilization and education. Soldiers on the other hand, only have one job. While politicians stabilize, soldiers neutralize.

Stabilization and neutralization are polar opposites. A single entity, or organization like the military, cannot perform both of these acts simultaneously. It's a disaster waiting to happen, not only in principle, but in the minds of the individuals attempting it. There is simply too much gray area between these polar opposites for a single mind to deal with. How can we ask our young men and women to love thy neighbor as thyself and give out charity to the masses one day, and the next day pull the trigger?

Trying to perform one's duty while simultaneously conforming to both of these poles breeds guilt. The guilt associated, when these things are no longer painted in black and white, plays havoc within a soldier's moral resiliency. This guilt is Post Traumatic Stress Disorder (PTSD) just waiting to manifest itself.

PTSD is a mental disorder that can develop after a person is exposed to a traumatic event, such as combat, or other threats on a person's life. It can be a silent and sometimes deadly disorder, and its progression is far from being fair.

Methods used to categorize humanity such as race, religion, creed, status, ethnicity, gender, the list goes on… do not exist in a foxhole. If God created all men, Samuel Colt made all men equal. (Colt is considered to be the father of modern day firearms.) Perceived social inequities do not exist when the possibility of death is forefront. Even in the uneducated and bigoted, these categorical ideas are nonexistent when bullets fly.

The astounding majority of U.S. military members have accepted their brothers and sisters as they are. We do not even consider these categories of humanity. As a White, Christian, blue collar man, I am equivalent to a Black, Muslim, white collar woman, as my fellow sister in arms. We are human and military members, nothing else matters to the lot of us. The military is the only institution on the face of the planet where complete acceptance when the shit hits the fan, is fully understood.

Leave us be, and let us be proud. Stop taking away my edge.

I PRESENT to you, Jennifer, my solution to the world's problems. I opened a can of worms in the previous rant. Presenting issues is just simply complaining if no solution is offered. So if I were Czar for the day I'd give the world this gift. It's possibly a solution to all of our problems.

THE ASSHOLE LAW

The fact that the Ku Klux Klan, or any other hate group for that matter, publicly exists in America in the 21st century is gut wrenching to me. Americans have indeed come a long way, but we still have a ways to go. If a participating member of one of these hate groups will not allow themselves to be persuaded by reasonable argument into beliefs that are contrary to their organization's spewed hatred, they are forever labelled an asshole in my book. Period!

I can say without a doubt in my mind that my fellow military brothers and sisters would agree with me. We have no tolerance for these types of assholes within our ranks. We don't have the time or the energy for any ridiculous bullshit hatred of men. Few persons, no matter their profession, would deny that people involved with hate groups are in fact assholes. But yet America seems to allow them to flourish. What in the hell are we doing?

People should not be allowed to be assholes in public, toward the public, or toward another human being. People should also not be allowed to break promises, include fine print clauses, or be blatantly deceitful toward another human being. That's the behavior of an asshole.

These types of behaviors are often blamed on organizations. Like, "the factory where I worked stole my pension." No, the factory is a building… assholes stole your pension. Organizations and corporations are made up of people. America is made up of people, and Americans are allowed to be assholes.

If I were Czar for the day I would permanently simplify the law books and create one common law of the land. I present to you… "The Asshole Law".

Miriam Webster Dictionary definition of asshole:
1. *usually vulgar*: anus
2. a. *usually vulgar*: a stupid, annoying, or detestable person
   b. *usually vulgar*: the least attractive or desirable part or area -used in phrases like *asshole of the world*

There is no written law against being an asshole. In fact over the course of our young country's existence, elected lawmakers have written genuine excuses allowing people to be assholes directly into the law books. None of the books of law studied by hopeful lawyers prior to the Bar exam actually bars asshole behavior. The written law can actually provide the very pathway for it. It is completely legal for Americans to be assholes. Again, what in the hell are we doing?

For instance let's look at a large corporation's Board of Executives that legally steals employee's pensions through loopholes written into IRS code. The Asshole Law would ensure that these board members would be convicted of being Executive Assholes. Their sentence: life of writing simplified IRS tax code, and paying each employee back double what was stolen from their promised pensions. Found under Asshole Law Article 17, Business Executive Dickhead Section 2 of Anus Appendix 1.8-12. Czar pounds his gavel. Case closed.

The IRS loophole writers in cahoots with these Executive Assholes are also assholes punishable under Asshole Law. They'd be convicted of being Public Service Assholes, a horrible kind of asshole. And secondly be convicted of being Business Executive Dickhead Accomplices. Their sentence: 10 years, no vacation taken or accrued, and assisting the Business Executive Dickheads with writing a new simplified tax code. They could now all be asshole cronies for the greater good, not for greed and selfishness. These types of assholes don't stand a chance under Asshole Law.

Let's look at laying off employees from a factory and buying an island in the Bahamas. Person(s) are instantly convicted of Executive

Assholistic Behavior. Sentence: 5 years working for minimum wage at the factory, paying everyone they laid off an executive salary and giving them residence on the island.

People who write and approve laws that entice corporations to move businesses to foreign countries would be convicted of being Wellbeing of Working Americans Assholes, and convicted secondly of being Publicly Elected Government Assholes, the worst asshole infraction possible. They'd also receive a third conviction of being Business Executive Dickhead Accomplices. The latter two types of assholes typically go hand in hand. Sentence: life with no chance of any pension other than Social Security, and mandatory utilization of the Affordable Care Act website for health insurance.

Actually moving a business to a foreign country strictly for greed and excess profit would also be punishable under Asshole Law.

Furthermore:
Being a white racist asshole. Sentence: 5 years living in Section 8 housing in South Chicago. Being a black racist asshole. Sentence: 5 years living in trailer park in rural West Virginia. Being any type of racist asshole is considered being an asshole. Gathering as racist assholes in public, or looting and destroying property while claiming racism as motive, are examples of being assholes and would all be punishable under The Asshole Law.

Cellular companies advertising $49.99 for a plan and having hidden monthly fees of $23.57, cable TV companies charging 15 dollars more every year while maintaining the same contract, hotdogs sold in any other quantity than that of a pack of hotdog buns, Veterans Affairs (VA) social workers who don't listen to the pleas of their patients, and soldiers who are deployed to the middle of the bone dry desert and leave the water running full blast the entire time they are shaving while I watch my tax dollars go down the drain. All of them are assholes.

An individual who files for custody of a child only after a child support order has been issued. Asshole. A father who was not present for the first years of a child's life. Also an asshole. An individual who records a conversation without consent, and uses specific parts of the conversation in court for their benefit. Asshole. Or someone who files a lawsuit for anything absurd like spilling hot coffee on themselves. Asshole. A parent who files a lawsuit because their child was injured on a neighborhood trampoline is also an asshole. Or someone who files a malpractice suit against a Dr. after signing the risk paperwork, therefore driving up everyone else's insurance rates. Asshole.

The court system that grants said custody or monetary settlement to any of these "victims", are all assholes of the worst kind. Or the lawyer who takes on any of these cases, represents the victims, and wins the lawsuits… bigtime asshole.

Parents who threaten a Little League Umpire after every single call that didn't go the way of their child's team would be immediately convicted of being a General Asshole in Public. Their sentence: 2 years serving as Little League Umpire, beginning immediately. The former Umpire would instantaneously take off his protective gear and hand it over to the General Asshole in Public and new Little League Umpire, in the middle of the inning. I'll bet that'd make assholes think twice before being an asshole.

Any fast food corporation's sandwich menu photo appearing as if there is an entire side of beef, mouthwateringly slow roasted, or a giant grilled hamburger patty on the sandwich. While salivating in expectations of grandeur, I cannot even see the meat under the bun on the actual sandwich I am given. Assholes. Corporation's sentence: taking a photo of the very last sandwich served, and using it to advertise on their damn menu board.

In the military we cannot afford to be assholes to one another. If a soldier is an asshole, he/she won't last too long. We are ultimately a team and must be cohesive in all our practices. Being a cohesive team is drilled into every single one of us from day one. Most of us have heard the saying, "there is no I in team". Well, there is no asshole in team either. Although it does sometimes occur, generally we refrain from assholistic behavior within our ranks. Our lives may one day depend on it.

Apart from the military however, the list of legal ways to be an asshole in America goes on infinitely. Soldiers don't need forced social idealism and help from lawmakers in order to help us refrain from being assholes. That very experiment is what got us here in the first place.

Again, leave us be, and let us be proud. Stop taking away my edge.

Jesus said "Love thy neighbor as thyself." Asshole Law has same intention, it's just stated a little differently. "Don't be an asshole!"

All in favor of The Asshole Law say, "Aye-sshole".

DELIVERING STUFF we cannot identify, to people we cannot reveal, to places we cannot designate, in a fight we cannot discuss. It's what military logisticians do, but it's not the stuff of legend. Legend is born of the warfighter on the front lines, living in the dirt, fighting twice as many bad guys, while living on a half canteen of water, no food, 120 rounds of ammunition and their M4 carbine weapon.

It is the logistician's job to supply that warfighter, and the legwork of supplying the warfighter from behind the scenes can often go unrewarded. Working day after long day diligently completing tasks, rarely seeing results, and not being able to discuss any of it with loved ones, has always been frustrating to me.

But, without the logistician's delivery of stuff we will not identify, to people we will not reveal, to places we will not designate, in a fight we will not discuss, we fail. It's "POG" stuff of legend. I will explain.

Legend or not, I think you'll enjoy this next story, Jen.

THE GOOD IDEA FAIRY

The military has an acronym for everything, so I will refer to the Air Base in this story as MAB. "Mysterious Air Base" was strategically located somewhere in the southern Arabian Peninsula. It stood in stark contrast to the various combat centric Army hell holes I had been sent to over my career. MAB consisted of several large rigid tents, around 300 mobile two man trailers for living quarters, and a huge aircraft runway. It was home to a few enormous C-17 cargo jets that hauled cargo to and from Afghanistan.

As the Taliban seemed to have retreated into thin air, our mission at MAB was the retrograde (return) of U.S. cargo from Afghanistan and downsizing U.S. efforts there. In return for the use of the runway, a handful of fighter aircraft were given to the host country's Air Force.

The U.S. had a small detail of pilots and mechanics that trained their pilots and performed maintenance on the aircraft. Presence of those aircraft were among the many diplomatic mysteries a soldier learns simply by being in the right place at the right time.

MAB's mission was definitely a POG mission. POG stands for People Other than Grunts, and can be a derogatory term used by members of the military who are actually doing the fighting to convey their opinion of the unimportance of everyone else's mission.

It's important here to point out the three main categories of Army jobs. They are specialized combat arms (Special Forces), combat arms (grunts), and people other than grunts (POG's). All military personnel are taught the "basic" combat skills of a soldier at Basic Training. Combat is the military's main mission, but most POG's never see combat.

Although the mission at MAB was certainly not the stuff of legend or what movies are made of, it was nonetheless extremely important to the making of the movie as a whole. The fact of the matter is that without POG's, the warfighters would not last very long. Warfighters, combat arms soldiers, or grunt types can only carry a certain amount of supplies on their backs. Without replacement fuel, food, water, ammunition, etc., they would only last a few days on the battlefield. Although they'd never admit to that out loud.

> Jen, I know these things because I was a warfighter/combat arms soldier for the first thirteen years of my career and I'd never admit it back then either. As a proud POG during the second half of my career, I knew what the combat side of the military looked like. My own warfighter stories will surface later.

MAB was full of POGs, myself included, and was comparable to a small resort town with very little going on and way too many homeowner association rules. There were a ton of "town hall" meetings used as a platform to discuss issues and express opinions, but without any ability to take action on them.

Americans, including its military personnel do not seem to have the ability to accept things as they are. If we would just step back and take a look at our current situation, most of us would come to the conclusion that things are pretty darn good. We have a lot to be grateful for. The same was true at MAB.

I mentioned in a previous story that in order for something to be deemed unfair, it requires a comparison. Being a combat arms soldier for the first half of my military career has given me the insight for a proper comparison between a combat deployment and my POG deployment at MAB. Things were pretty darn good at MAB compared to combat. Although, I suppose nearly everything is pretty darn good compared to combat.

The point is that if we were in the heat of battle at MAB, the homeowner association meetings would have never taken place. The gripes at these meetings were trivial, and were considered ridiculous by most of us who had previously seen combat.

One of the many ridiculous homeowner association rules, created by U.S. military POGs, has to do with the proper wear of safety glasses.

It seems like half of today's required Army training consists of safety training. Wearing safety glasses is important for safety purposes, and in the military we are well aware of proper safety precautions. The personnel at MAB, however, were not operating pneumatic nail guns, running chainsaws or boring out the stock headers in a 69 Pontiac GTO. Nor were we "in combat". Only a very few of the Air Force Security Forces were even carrying their weapons. But we all had to wear our safety glasses… all the damn time.

My personal combat zone attire, during off duty hours at MAB, included shorts and a bright Hawaiian shirt with flowers. As a constant accessory to my fashionable wartime ensemble I was also required to wear my safety glasses. That's right, I wore a Hawaiian shirt at least three evenings a week, and at the same time was required to wear safety glasses. It was a silly POG rule.

It would have made perfect sense to be wearing safety glasses if we were all in full combat gear, complete with vest and helmet, due to the threat of an enemy attack. But we were not. While at MAB, I never even took that gear out of my duffel bags.

All branches of the military have adopted the manlier name "eye protection" in safety glasses' stead. At the risk of sounding paisley myself, I'll take this one manlier step further and use the military abbreviation for eye protection. EyePro.

> Jennifer, throughout my entire career, whenever anyone has said "EyePro" I have always had the image of a cape wearing optometrist superhero with thick horned rimmed glasses in a red speedo pop into my head. While I was at MAB, the optometrist superhero sat on my shoulder, and constantly reminded me to wear my EyePro.

Army Regulation 670-1 is the written standard for wear and appearance of the military uniform. Regulation is reality in the military and we have a library full of regulations. This particular regulation states in some form or another that: only prescription eyeglasses will be worn while indoors, and eyeglasses of any form will not be seen on the exterior of the uniform, unless they are being properly worn over your eyeballs.

So... I can't hang my EyePro from a lanyard, I can't attach them to my uniform, I can't prop them on my forehead ...but I'm required to have them on me at all times. Therefore, the only option to ensure that our EyePro stays with us while we are not wearing them, is to stuff them into a cargo pocket. Because of a lack of options due to a POG regulation, soldiers have sat on and crunched EyePro at a frequency equal to saltine crackers destined for a bowl of Uncle Eddie's chili on Super Bowl Sunday.

Over my career I have personally forgotten my EyePro on a helicopter, in several vehicles, on a Boeing 777 passenger jet in Qatar, and on my lunch tray. I've also smashed several pairs. One pair of my EyePro was smashed in a cargo pocket while I was being smashed in between two equally smashed soldiers. Amid all of this nonsense, the optometrist superhero just laughed at me, and reminded me to wear my EyePro.

If I could have simply propped my EyePro on my forehead, or dangled them around my neck, I may have saved the taxpayer $200 dollars or more over my career. I know I am not alone.

A favorite saying among soldiers is that these types of rules, among all things bizarre and unreasonable, are brought to you by the "Good Idea Fairy". The "Good Idea Fairy" is a mostly invisible, but oh so very influential, guide. She lives across the globe, somewhere on a magical island where "good ideas" are born. At the flick of her wand, military decision makers are instantly smitten when she places a good idea in their heads.

Soldiers don't dare question the Good Idea Fairy, or have opinions on her intentions. Questioning her is not worth the effort, because most of us already know that the reason for her rule's existence does not exist. What?

Read those sentences again, because there may be no statement in the history of military historical hysteria that can be expressed with more certainty. The rules exist, but the reason for them may not. Who's on first? We all just simply nod our heads in a north and south direction, get onboard and prepare ourselves for the wild ride.

Good Idea Fairies have the ability to manifest themselves in many ways. Sometimes they come to life as a make-believe Fairy. These flying gremlins are quite difficult to deal with. Usually they land on the nose of an unsuspecting victim as a "good idea" before the victim even knows the Fairy is around.

It is not uncommon to have a flyswatter that is labelled the "Good Idea Fairy Swatter" in any military office. While I was at MAB, we would kill off a few Fairies each day in an attempt at eradication before catastrophe, but they just kept on coming.

A question that I sometimes ponder is: does a vessel, christened the "Good Idea Ferry" actually transport an entire army of Good Idea Fairies?

POG... I personally do not use that term derogatorily. The Army is one cohesive team, and there is no I in team. There is no asshole in team either. In fact, the entire U.S. military is one cohesive team! In this story I will share a couple awesome experiences I have had while working with the other branches of service.

DIVINE BOVINE

As one of four Army Soldiers among the Air Force Airmen, MAB was truly a little slice of deployment heaven for me. Recliners, pool tables, Nautilus gym equipment, air conditioning that actually worked, sand volleyball, gourmet chow and chow hall, are comforts that the Air Force does better than any other branch of service.

Every single Wednesday, we were served a true bovine masterpiece for evening chow. A bovine masterpiece compared to those served at a picnic table at Grandpa's over Memorial Day weekend. It was pretty damn impressive considering I was 6700 miles from Grandpa's, and had not seen a cow in a year. Maybe we were actually eating camel? I didn't care, the steaks were fantastic. Either way, right before my eyes was a close knit group of sizzling T-bone steaks grilling ever so nicely over glowing charcoal briquettes. One of the inch thick, beautiful bone-in slices was being cooked medium rare, especially for me.

At 16:30 sharp, you could smell the freshly lit charcoal smoke wafting its way throughout the confines of the base. The standing joke was that if the enemy couldn't see us, they certainly could smell us, especially on Wednesdays. The meal was completed with potato salad or coleslaw, green beans, buttermilk biscuits, a tall glass of milk, and a slice of pie ala mode. And if you asked nicely you could have both potato salad and coleslaw. Embracing those little things is what gets a soldier through an entire year away from home.

Air Force chow halls typically even have actual silverware and plates, complimented by a real, reusable glass for your drink of choice. All of which is impressive in comparison to Army chow halls, where breaking the plastic knife in an attempt to cut the piece of shoe leather served as a steak, or drinking from a leaking paper cup made by the lowest bidder is commonplace. I've munched on tines of a plastic fork many times. All Army soldiers have. Not while dining with the Air Force, though. They do amenities right.

On one particular Wednesday evening, Lucas, AKA "Briar", was one of four guys in shorts and flowered Hawaiian shirts grilling our T-bones. Briar completed his stylish attire with a white apron printed with an enormous green largemouth bass that held grilling utensils, and of course, his EyePro. Thank goodness Briar had on his EyePro, because grilling tongs and T-bones are inherently dangerous, and have been known to cause blindness.

The nickname, Briar, fit him perfectly. It stemmed from his southern Ohio/West Virginian accent, and the fact that he was known to be rough around the edges. His stories of bar fights and being picked up by the Military Police (MP's) in Germany years ago, top any I've ever heard. His nickname also fit perfectly with the way he struck the ball during the Wednesday evening sand volleyball games. He served the ball by taking an uncoordinated crooked leap, while swinging an overly flexed arm overhead. He worked on those arms daily at the gym. When he served the ball, it had the same amount of spin as a serve from a ping pong master, and it was hilarious to watch. It was quite effective 50% of the time. The other half of the time Briar's volleyball serve ended up in the briars.

Even though he was cooking a steak for me at the moment, and I was on a first name basis with him, I couldn't procure my T-bone from Briar. I had forgotten my EyePro, and that was a NO-GO. Good Idea Fairies trump any progressive way of thinking brought to the dinner table. So, I headed 500 yards back to my living quarters for my EyePro, and thirty minutes later I was finally served a steak, grilled medium rare to my liking. The blackened lines that Briar created on that T-Bone were a far cry from the boiled cube steaks soaked in fake A1 steak sauce that were served to the masses at Army bases across the Middle East. Thank you, Air Force, for the great weekly bovine grilling extravaganza.

Nearly the entire base showed up for sand volleyball after each Wednesday's evening feast. It truly was the only show in town. Nobody wanted to man the machine gun towers located on the base perimeter on Wednesdays. MAB's Commanding Officer was a 6 foot 5 former Louisiana State University (LSU) volleyball player. Needless to say, we played a lot of volleyball.

The "Top Gun" movie means way more to the Air Force than it ever will to the Army. But, there was honestly some resemblance between us and that shirtless volleyball clip in the movie. The one that womenfolk all go batty over. There was nothing else to do during time off but exercise and play volleyball. We were all in phenomenal physical shape and had our dog tags on. Fitness is paramount on military bases during deployments. More so than any other place on the planet.

The games played on, through dusk and into early darkness. Laughter was commonly heard at MAB, well into the late hours of the evening. Except for my constant yearning to take Isaac and Isaiah fishing back home, life wasn't so bad most days. The Air Force, and all personnel on MAB, made the most out of what we had.

While at MAB my Army cohorts and I had been trying to come up with a fitting name for Mysterious Air Base. Something fun, that worked well and slid off the tongue easily. I tried to call it Club Med, but when I mentioned Club Med the young kids didn't even know what Club Med was. Before I left MAB, we began referring to MAB as "Mayberry", from the Andy Griffith show.

Mayberry had a true small town feel to it, and it even had a silly Sheriff to escort someone home if needed. Playing the part of silly Sheriff were the Air Force Security Forces. In good natured, military branch competition, we Army soldiers formed a pact with the few Marines on base, and ganged up on the Security Forces. Outnumbered by a longshot, our group of ground troops still took every opportunity to express how our branch was obviously superior to the Air Force.

It was our responsibility to not so gently let the Air Force know that on the ground, they were kind of like having a wiener dog for protection at the junk yard. You know there is something there, but once you hear it bark and recognize it's not a Rottweiler, some loss of credibility washes over the situation. Don't get me wrong. That little dog has a great heart, but showing force eye to eye is a much better task for the Army or the Marines. It's what we do. Although I suppose any group of camouflaged people strapped with M4 carbines is intimidating. The Security Forces were the only ones at MAB with weapons.

When deciding how exactly to pick on any given military branch, a soldier must choose his ammunition wisely. For instance, it's generally not a good idea to get into a long distance rucksack marching competition with a U.S. Marine. Marines walk everywhere, and carry everything needed for a few days on their backs. Their fitness standards are the highest among all the military branches. They are the very best at what they are designed to do.

Being the guy that I am, I accepted a rucksack challenge from a Marine Gunnery Sergeant while we were both at MAB. He destroyed me. Gunny could have carried both of our packs and me for the last mile of our hike, and he still would have won the race. I accepted the challenge, but never really expected to win the race. Not a rucksack marching competition against a Marine.

Acknowledgement of different branch strengths is acceptable. We are different, and do have different strengths. Admitting to another branch that they have such strengths is a completely different story.

Recognizing one of our strengths as ground pounders, the Air Force Security Forces would utilize the few Army soldiers and the couple Marines at MAB as training partners. They asked us the question, "How would we attack MAB if we were the bad guys?"

We (Army and Marines) devised plans to "infiltrate" the small base while the Air force would "protect it". We assisted the Air Force with counter attack measures, identifying weak perimeter points, and various other tactical issues. The plans we devised were very intricate and were top notch training for us and the Security Forces. The training was conducted in preparation for worst case scenario attacks, which fortunately never occurred.

The Security Forces did a great job. I learned from them, as they learned from me. As a soldier, I sure as hell wasn't going to admit that to them. They accepted my ribbings with good nature, and returned fire appropriately.

It's always interesting to work with the other branches of service. The Air Force and the Marines at MAB were true professionals, and it was an honor to serve alongside them. This would hold true throughout my career.

One of the Marines I met on MAB was a "boot" (recent "boot camp" graduate). He was still young and innocent. If he had ever put a razor to his face, he caught the two fuzzy whiskers that may or may not have actually been there. I cannot remember his name, but I remember he was from Wyoming County, New York and his father somehow worked indirectly with my uncle. It is strange how you meet people on the other side of the world and find some oddball connection to them.

After exchanging normal formalities he told me that he was on his way into Afghanistan with his new unit. This was his first assignment. He was not yet nineteen years old, and mentioned his birthday was next week. I then realized my original enlistment date into the United States Army was a few months prior to when this kid was born. The look I gave him in that instant must have been priceless. I had been in the Army longer than this kid had been on Earth. Drive on soldier.

MAB probably doesn't sound all that bad. It really wasn't. Part of me actually misses Mayberry, with all of its idiosyncrasies. It was a great deployment. Even with the POG rules.

The aspects of MAB that we would like to truly escape, like the Good Idea Fairy, seem to follow soldiers wherever they go while serving in the military. Anywhere we go, military personnel struggle to obtain clarification and secondary information from their leaders, who struggle to obtain information from their leaders, and on up the ladder. We want to know why, but typically we never find that answer. So we continue our duty to get the job done, without those answers.

Most of the time not another word is spoken, we maintain radio silence…

IV

Significant Silence,
Considering the Significance

BEFORE I became a logistics POG, during the first thirteen years of my military career, I was a Combat Engineer. Those years included a combat deployment to Iraq. This deployment did not consist of niceties such as flowered shirts, medium rare T-bones, volleyball games or the comforts of the Air Force. 2004 in its entirety, was a year full of violent and completely life changing experiences.

Now that we have covered all the essentials and a few nonessentials as well, the remaining letters to you, Jennifer, will follow the sequential timetable of my life when considering my time in Iraq. In these letters, we'll journey together through the preparation for my deployment to Iraq, the high peaks and low valleys, the humanity, and the aftermath.

These next couple letters cover preparing for war, prior to actually stepping onto Iraqi soil. Once again we'll begin on September 11th, 2001. Since that day my bags have never been unpacked.

BOHICA, A PREREQUISITE FOR WAR

In response to the attacks on American soil on Sept 11th, 2001, I left my job building homes and volunteered to be a Department of Homeland Security, uniformed and armed guard at Wright Patterson (Wright Pat) Air Force base in Dayton, Ohio. Extra security was required on most government installations during the aftermath of 9/11, while patriotism was at an all-time high in our proud and grieving country.

After the twin towers fell, Operation Enduring Freedom was the name given to the large scale military operation that began during President George W. Bush's tenure. Operation Enduring Per-Diem was the nickname that eventually labeled the new Department of Homeland Security mission for which I had volunteered. The nickname stuck because most of us would receive a daily per diem stipend to eat and stay near the respective facilities where we would be working. After three physicals, seven vaccinations, and 1000 PowerPoint slide presentations pertaining to various factions of homeland security, I was deemed "fit for duty" as an armed security guard.

It was a good job for the short time that I had it, and the per diem money was great. But it didn't last long. In early 2003 rumors of an oncoming deployment among the Ohio Army Engineers began to circulate. The formal word came about four months prior to the publishing of the official deployment orders. I was pulled from the Department of Homeland Security mission in late July to assist with pre-deployment training, and officially ordered to report on December 19th, 2003 to go to war in Iraq. I was not assigned to deploy with my own unit from Norwalk, Ohio, but with another National Guard unit from Portsmouth, Ohio.

> Jennifer, throughout our time together, you have no doubt learned many lessons at a Soldiering 101 level. You are about to get a lesson from a Soldiering 400 level class. Tying the Good Idea Fairy together with the Green Weenie, and an explanation of the path to BOHICA is the stuff of military doctoral dissertations. Before reading on, prepare yourself!

The unfortunate moment when a soldier recognizes they are about to get screwed is referred to as "BOHICA" (pronounced bo-he-ca). I was supposed to be coming home every night after pulling a security shift as a glorified gate keeper at Wright Patterson Air Force Base, and earning a nice daily per diem to boot. Nope! Now I was headed to war in Iraq with a group of hillbillies from Portsmouth, Ohio. That moment of reversal of fortune, when my good paying job instantly turned into going to war, was a BOHICA moment. It's the military version of Murphy's Law. BOHICA is an acronym for Bend Over, Here It Comes Again.

The U.S. Army somehow manages to muck up everything comfortable, luxurious, tasty, sexy, and relaxing. The only reason that life was good at Mysterious Air Base (MAB) was because MAB was run by the Air Force! I am 100% certain that the Army would have succeeded in making my time at MAB somewhat miserable. The steaks would have been broiled, not grilled. Even the volleyball games would have in some way or another, been crappy. If there is too much fun being had, or too much relaxation, the Army inevitably muddles the smiles. The U.S. Army can amazingly manifest misery. The following illustrates this concept perfectly.

"You have time to write letters home, SFC Capell?" asked the Army. "Get a detail of six soldiers together to wash the tents. The General ordered it last week. Begin the wash detail tomorrow!" yelled the U.S. Army.

"But Sir, there is a nasty sandstorm headed this way!" I pleaded to no avail.

"Suck it up buttercup! General Overtidy ordered us to wash the tents, and we are already a week late!" was Lieutenant Soapinbucket's response to my plea.

He was told by Major Sponge that, "The tents needed washing yesterday!"

Colonel Kleen, Major Sponge's boss, told him that, "The tents need washing now!"

Colonel Kleen thought he overheard General Overtidy say, "Wash the tents!" a month ago.

But what the General actually said was, "My Father and I used to go fishing every spring in the Adirondacks in upstate New York. The dirty fabric tents across the Middle East remind me of the old canvas tent that my father used to make me wash after every trip."

The words "tent", "the", and "wash" were present within that nice story about the General's childhood, but there is no real reason to wash tents in the middle of the desert. The Good Idea Fairy had struck again.

Valuing my career, my only possible reply to Lieutenant Soapinbucket was, "Yes Sir, wash the tents… got it."

Tent washing during a sandstorm was an actual event that I participated in. In this case, not only did the Army manage to ruin my good time, it took several of my comrades along for the ride, too. "Strength in numbers", and "misery loves company" are two phrases with which veterans are quite familiar. How in the world did writing letters home somehow morph down a miserable road into washing tents in a sandstorm? BOHICA, that's how.

Insert any pleasurable experience here _____, and the Army will somehow manage to screw it up. The U.S. Army is the alarm clock to a sex dream. It is Bill Buckner's between the legs error, extending the Red Sox curse. It is John Elway's 80 yard touchdown drive with 53 seconds left on the clock, for a Cleveland Browns fan. Or a traffic jam on the way to the job interview of a lifetime.

While BOHICA is the realization of bad times ahead, the actual destroyer of good times is referred to as the "Green Weenie". If life is good at the moment, soldiers had better take heed! If things are going well, the Green Weenie is surely lurking around the next corner and will make itself known momentarily.

The Green Weenie manifests itself in the form of a large green dick. Green for Army, and dick for... well, a dick. An invisible dick, but nonetheless felt by soldiers everywhere. Soldiers can't get screwed into miserable endeavors without a dick, right? So we invented one to blame the bad times on. Yes, we sophomorically invented a giant, green, imaginary dick that we could blame for turning our good times into catastrophes.

The Soldier 400 level cliff notes are as follows.
1. Good Idea Fairies create the ideas for misery.
2. BOHICA (Bend Over Here It Comes Again) is the moment when a soldier understands they are now going to be miserable.
3. The Green Weenie, is the implementer of said misery.

Such is the life of an unfortunate soldier. And such was my life at the instant I realized I was going to war in Iraq for a year, instead of making daily per diem money at Wright Pat in Dayton, Ohio. A good job, making great money, had somehow morphed into going off to war. The Green Weenie had gotten me. BOHICA!

ALONG WITH a few other soldiers from my home unit of Charlie Company 612th Battalion of Combat Engineers (explosives and demolitions) from Norwalk, Ohio, I was cross-leveled to deploy to Iraq with Bravo Company 216th Battalion of Construction Engineers (roads, concrete, life structure and facilities) from Portsmouth, Ohio. Cross-leveling is the National Guard's way of filling vacancies in a deploying unit. It makes sense for a unit to deploy at 100% manpower or slightly greater. Pulling soldiers from other units to fill vacancies is still the solution today.

SIGNIFICANCE

On December 19th 2003, I reported to Portsmouth, Ohio. I had never met any of the guys from Bravo Company before, but would become lifelong friends with many of them. Fellow members of my former unit and I were forced to integrate quickly. I am fairly certain I could be placed anywhere on earth and make friends, so I enjoyed being one of the new guys in town. Eventually, I'd become a leader and well-respected cohort among these new found friends.

Jennifer, at this time in my life I was in my physical prime, strong, and quick witted. I was a recent college graduate, a former Wittenberg University Tiger swim team captain, and I would not back down or slow down. I had life by the horns during those few years after college and prior to this deployment. It really was a great time to be Joel A. Capell. I was going places, and I knew it. My peers and superiors respected me and valued my opinions.

There were about 130 soldiers in Bravo Company, which was divided into four platoons. Each platoon had around 35 soldiers who were broken up into four or five squads within the platoon. I was one of five soldiers in 3rd platoon with the grade of E-6. But even though I was a Staff Sergeant, I was not in a Squad Leader position. I was actually slotted into an E-4 position. I was getting paid two full grades higher than the position in which I was placed.

In Iraq, this placement would add some additional requirements to my mission, some unwanted and some I relished. When the 216th Engineers were tasked with a mission requiring E-6 leadership, my name was consistently on the top of the list because I was not assigned as the leader of a 216th squad of Engineers. As a squad leader, I had no squad. This did cause a few issues between me and some peers during the months that led up to us entering Iraq. When it became understood that having an actual squad of soldiers would keep them from being tasked out on some of the more dangerous missions during our tenure, those issues quickly disappeared.

The 216th Engineer Battalion was comprised of heavy equipment operators and various types of Construction Engineers. Our main missions in Iraq would be creating fortifications for force protection by pushing up earth berms, and building structures for living and working. Bulldozers, scrapers, graders, dump trucks, tractor trailers to haul it all, and various HMMWV (High Mobility Multipurpose Wheeled Vehicle) or "hummers" would all be a part of our daily missions.

With all this heavy equipment in the Middle Eastern desert, we would literally be playing in the world's largest sandbox.

Jennifer, to give you an idea of how much equipment the 216th Engineers had, it was said that if we had driven every piece of equipment north out of Kuwait into Iraq, we would have been the largest continuous combat zone convoy in the history of U.S. military operations. The first vehicle would have reached Bagdad by the time the last one crossed the border out of Kuwait. That tactic would have been a slow moving target for countless miles of ambushes waiting to happen, and slightly suicidal.

The 216th Engineer Battalion would be supplying the next four to seven years' worth of engineering equipment to central Iraq with our National Guard equipment from Ohio. We didn't bring a single piece of it home with us. The next group of deploying engineers would fall in on our equipment, which actually made sense to us and the taxpayer, a seemingly rare occurrence during the war.

As part of our pre-deployment training, the U.S. Army paid First Army (Active Duty Army training branch) personnel to travel to Portsmouth, Ohio to teach us Improvised Explosive Device (IED) evasion tactics. We were taught that the most dangerous mission in this war was getting from point A to point B, and were trained to drive fast and to keep moving at all costs. The best tactics to avoid IED's and ambush were speed and maneuverability. So that is what we trained to do.

Military vehicles of the time were not designed for speed and maneuverability. And with all the heavy engineering equipment we would have loaded on tractor trailers, we could literally forget about speed and maneuverability. It seemed silly to train for something that couldn't actually happen, but that is exactly what we did. BOHICA! With this type of pre-deployment training we were setting ourselves up to be ripe for the picking by the Green Weenie. We might as well just have assumed the position.

We weren't training from tacit knowledge for engineers. The war was at its inception, there were no lessons learned from experience on which to base the training. We took part in the cookie cutter pre-deployment training program that had just been established. The fact that the Army paid individuals to teach us how to go-cart around corners in dump trucks was illogical and downright foolish. All the way from the Pentagon, the Good Idea Fairy had struck again.

Suck it up buttercup! Drive on soldier! So that's what we did. We drove on, silently and slowly around the corners.

After learning our go-cart driving techniques and completing IED evasion and equipment training in Portsmouth, we laboriously loaded everything onto flatbed railroad cars, conscientiously strapping it all down. Possibly the most famous saying from Special Operations Green Beret's is "slow is smooth, and smooth is fast". This means slowing down and being smooth and efficient, or without mishap during an operation is much faster than the alternative. Mishap has a higher percentage of occurring when hurrying, and nothing about heavy equipment operations is quick. Our equipment would journey slowly and smoothly via train, to Norfolk Virginia. Then it would be deliberately loaded onto vessels for shipment to the Middle East.

Many tears were shed as we said goodbye to family and friends for the fourteen month separation. It was certainly tough on everyone. I gave a final hug to my then wife (whom I will call Fi), and we were off to Atterbury Training Base to prepare for desert operations training.

This training occurred during one of the coldest January's ever recorded in Edinburg, Indiana. We arrived January 2nd, 2004, and it was absolutely frigid over the entire month we were there. While it was 90 degrees in Iraq, and 95 in Kuwait, it was negative 20 degrees in Indiana. It was so cold that we started fires at our training sites for warmth. The irony of needing snow suits and heavy gloves to train for the upcoming desert operations was laughable. We ended up carrying our heavy snow parkas, long underwear and snow pants with us the entire time we were deployed in Iraq. BOHICA!

The military and the U.S. populace as a whole was not prepared for the journey we were about to embark on. As the literal "tip of the spear" for ground occupation forces, neither were we. There were other military units who had deployed 6-9 months prior to us, but we would be the first wave of troops to arrive with large amounts of heavy earthmoving engineer equipment to the Iraqi Theatre of Operations. We were guinea pigs. Every unit at the time was cast into that role. Like them, we got more than our fair share of visits from the Green Weenie.

Other than the absurd temperatures, the only thing that I remember about the training at Atterbury was that it had very little to do with anything applicable in Iraq.

As a cross-leveled soldier, I didn't have the proper training certificate awarding me the title of Construction Engineer. I was trained as a demolitions or a Combat Engineer at Basic Training. Therefore, according to military doctrine, because I hadn't graduated "Army Construction Trades School" I did not possess the necessary skills to go to war as a Construction Engineer.

For this next bit of training, again the U.S. Army sent First Army training personnel. This time they were from Construction Engineer Basic Training, and were going to conduct a Construction Engineer school for us at Atterbury. Through this training, the 216th Engineer Battalion's newly cross-leveled soldiers would become 100% Construction Engineer qualified. Everyone must pass go, everyone would collect $200 worth of worthless monopoly money… and worthless training.

The instructors were by no means incompetent, they just simply didn't give a damn. Pissed off because they were told to come to frigid Indiana, I couldn't blame them. They evidently had given up hope, and were in a permanent BOHICA position. They were not the ones deploying, and probably recognized that the training they were offering us was somewhat ludicrous.

Being previously employed by a custom home builder/construction company, I knew more about the construction trades than the instructors. I was not alone in my knowledge. Many of us had worked in the skilled trades as civilians.

For our pre-deployment, "I'm going to war in Iraq" training, the other cross-leveled soldiers and I built four wooden framed, shingle roof, 10' x 14' storage sheds, complete with student fabricated trusses. We already possessed the required skills to craft the Taj Mahal of storage sheds, but lacked the proper Army Construction Engineer certification. Hell, we could have put a full bathroom and a furnace in them.

> Jennifer, since taking part in their construction, I have seen the storage sheds in all their majesty several times while on a weapons range at Atterbury. If for no other good reason at all, their existence provides fourteen, previously "untrained", but now current Army Construction Engineer certificate holders with a fantastic story about how they came into existence. To my knowledge these monumental feats of extraordinary engineering still occupy the Atterbury landscape.

I certainly hold some bias as a lifelong National Guard member, but my expectations of First Army's training in preparation for us to go to war, were not even close to being met. We were about to embark on an actual wartime mission. What in the hell were we doing building storage sheds? As a unit about to go to war, I expected to receive the proper training to do so. In my mind's eye, First Army was supposed to provide all of us with some awesome training and real life scenarios that would prepare us to fight Al-Qaeda.

I expected the full Sunday afternoon church potluck of Army training. Sampling 25 of Grandmother's stellar dishes, each one challenging my taste buds and my intellect as to how something could actually be this good. I knew apache attack helicopters were not going to land on the roof of the barracks at Atterbury, while escorted by B2 Stealth Bombers. But they should have! We should have painted our faces camouflage at zero dark thirty (0030, or thirty minutes past midnight), conducted our own jihad on the jihadists while fording the southern Indiana, Ohio River border into Kentucky during complete darkness, with full assault pack and loaded M16 rifles. I expected and thought we all deserved the Boeing 777 of capacity for training in preparation for a real war. Damn-it, we should have been given the ultimate preparation for the mental and physical toughness that would be required of us. My-o-my, was I ever wrong.

What in the hell... were we actually doing? We accomplished nothing over those seven weeks prior to leaving for war. What we did was not challenging or significant. The training provided by First Army in preparation for war was downright discouraging and disappointing to me.

The myth that National Guard soldiers were somehow inferior soldiers that had been instilled into my mind by my Basic Training Drill Sergeants had been debunked. In fact I came to see that the National Guard could actually run circles around the Active Army, in limited capacity. This would be confirmed repeatedly during the remaining years of my military service.

I do not want to take anything away from, or piss off my Active Duty brethren during this section of my letters. Active Duty combat arms units are the most skilled and powerful entity anywhere. In most instances they are better warriors than the National Guard and Reserves. Period, zero, zilch, nada, none, finite, no questions asked. This goes for my brethren in all branches of service. The Army, Navy, Air Force, Marines and Coast Guard active components train harder and more often. They are consistently in much better physical condition overall, and are forces to be reckoned with. They are built to fight, and do so with excellence. Active Duty combat arms units are paramount when it comes to actually "fighting" a war. Highly physical missions such as kicking down doors and operations that require massive amounts of training to be effective will always belong to them.

> Jen, this paragraph is an author's disclaimer. In my attempt to explain certain advantages the Guard and Reserves have over the Active component, take it with a grain of salt. Remember that the following may be more about life in general than about warfighting. Nonetheless, the next few paragraphs are truthful observations over my entire career.

An advantage that I see the National Guard having over the Active Duty Army is that we have a subject matter expert, in every subject. Our diversity makes us great. Need a banker? In addition to his military service, Captain Stocks happens to work for Chase Manhattan, Monday through Friday. What about a carpenter? Sergeant Builds works for the Carpenter's Local Union 123, and Lieutenant Blueprint runs a contracting business specializing in building homes. Nurses, retail, managers, cooks, engineers, electricians, school teachers, mechanics, you name it. In a large National Guard Battalion, there is bound to be an individual who works in nearly every profession.

The regular Army has entire units full of really good financial people, but there are no electricians in the mix. This makes the Active Army finance unit excellent at their actual job, but somewhat ineffective at anything else that might be thrown at them. Lack of diversity in skillset creates a somewhat ineffective force.

Another benefit is that a higher percentage of the National Guard has performed the very simple task of paying their water bill. The National Guard has a dose of real life that the Army simply does not have. The Army provides most of what is required for basic survival to its Active Duty members. Food, shelter, water, uniforms, etc., are provided. The Active Army affords a very simplistic lifestyle, where many things can be taken for granted.

In the Guard we all know that if you don't pay the water bill, you are soon to be without water. That knowledge provides drive and motivation to pay the water bill. Any smart person would then also attempt to conserve water throughout the month because the amount on the bill will reflect the usage.

Also a Guard member can and will be fired from our civilian jobs due to underperformance. It's tough to get fired from the Army. A soldier who "gets fired" from the Army will put more work into that task than he would by simply doing his job.

These pint-size things may seem overly simplistic, but these little life circumstances make a huge difference in an individual's drive, elevated expectations and performance standards. The Guard has simple motivators and life experience that the average Active Duty Army soldier may not.

I wouldn't have believed the Guard could possibly outperform the Active Army at tank driving without witnessing it with my own two eyes. During training at Fort Knox, Kentucky, the Ohio Guard's 145th Armored Regiment was in a friendly competition with a few Active Army units from an Armored Division. The competition consisted of four days of field maneuvers, tank operations and firing exercises. Ohio's 145th won the culminating event, the "Tank Tables". I will say that upon arriving at Fort Knox, the Active Duty units were ready the day they got there. The National Guard needed a few weeks to practice and hone in on the skillsets that they hadn't worked on in a while. If the "Tank Tables" competition had been the first week, the Guard would have certainly lost the friendly competition.

There are definitely differences between the Active and Reserve components. Take my opinions only for what they are. Civilian life and all its challenges create adaptation skills and incentives that motivate the Guard to succeed. And we typically do. If we don't succeed at first, we have the individual drive instilled within us to ensure that we will succeed the next time there is an opportunity to do so.

Let's get back to Atterbury and preparation for deployment. My first experience with the Active Duty Army outside of Basic Training was in preparation for the most important mission I would ever be a part of. In my opinion, going to a place where an enemy would be attempting to kill us was significant! In the nearly two months we had been on active duty orders in preparation to go to war, we built storage sheds for the National Guard in Indiana, froze our butts off during desert operations training, and became experts in speed and maneuverability IED evasion in ten ton dump trucks. All of that was completely useless, insignificant bullshit training.

Considering that a 10 ton dump truck has a 0 to 50 mph time of roughly two minutes, and the turning radius of a Beverly Hills estate, I now felt "overly prepared" for everything that Al-Qaeda could possibly throw at us. Not to mention the breathtaking storage sheds we put together were done so with the very finest craftsmanship. I'd have taken one home for my own backyard in a heartbeat! There was absolutely no use for them or the skills we trained on, in Iraq!

We learned absolutely nothing significant, considering the significance of our mission!

Drive on soldier, the Green Weenie patiently awaits. BOHICA! The ability to keep my mouth shut in regards to BOHICA ridiculousness and Good Idea Fairies was something that I learned from the Army while preparing for war. I was unable to see, then or now, how keeping the frustrations regarding these practices pent up would somehow be useful in any situation? Regardless, while preparing for war I learned to maintain radio silence.

In retrospect, the one thing I did learn from my time at Atterbury and other pre-deployment training experiences was that we got somewhat used to the not so gracious accommodations of deployment living. And we learned to live with each other. Prior to January 2004, the longest any of these men had spent together was a sixteen day Annual Training summer camp at Camp Grayling, Michigan.

Fistfights were not mandatory in order for our unit to become 100% approved with their pre-mobilization requirements. But, after 24 plus years in the Army, I will state that in order for a unit to be fully prepared and successful overseas, there needs to be a few fistfights prior to leaving. They're not in the official Army "deployment rule book", but fist fights and wrestling matches are part of the unwritten, Barracks School of Law training program. They need to take place before men and women are given weapons and live ammunition. For soldiers, fighting exercises the ego, subdues the ego, and creates a natural hierarchy. Fighting among each other creates the order of men.

We were obligated to come to terms with these basic sociological principles prior to leaving for the Middle East. And we had done so. It was finally time to go to war.

Greatest damn storage sheds ever built.
Built for WAR!

EVERY VETERAN who travelled overseas from early 2003 through November, 2015 will know exactly who I am writing about immediately after reading the title to this heartwarming story. The devotion and patriotism this woman showed to every single soldier who was boarding a plane to the Middle East at the embarkation and debarkation terminal, is a story that will remain in all of our hearts for our entire lives. Jennifer, there are tears in my eyes right now as I look up a photo of her to place into this letter home to you.

THE HUG LADY

Elizabeth Laird attended nearly every single deployment and homecoming in Fort Hood Texas from 2003, through 2015. Known to most of us veterans simply as the "Hug Lady", she would stand at the door as we walked out of the terminal in a single file line, and would give each of us a big hug before boarding the plane that would transport us to the Middle East. No matter how long it took, she would hug every single one of us. Even when her health began to deteriorate and she became unable to drive, she would catch a taxi to the terminal to hand out her dose of love to each and every one of us, both coming and going.

Many soldiers can recall the exact day when they received a hug from her, and still have the Psalm 91 card or the cross she handed them before their deployment. She was a devoted Christian who sought to give back. The Hug Lady was no doubt a woman who loved and was loved by God. Her hugs brought tears to many an eye. She gave over 500,000 hugs to servicemen and women over the course of twelve years. A half a million hugs! Even if it was well into the wee hours of the morning, she hugged us all when we left, and she hugged us again when we returned home.

Two of the crosses that hang from the rear view mirror of my car came from the Hug Lady. A feeble old woman standing at the door at 2:30 in the morning, minutes before I departed U.S. soil gave them to me, along with a warm and gentle hug. I was given a cross and two hugs in 2004-

2005, one going and one coming home. And another cross and two hugs in 2013-2014.

She spent the last two months of her life in the hospital. Her health declined quickly after her diagnosis of breast cancer. Nearly $100,000 dollars was raised toward her medical bills by veterans. During her last days in the hospital, soldiers from across the country travelled to Killeen, Texas to return the hug that she had once given them. There was an endless procession of veterans visiting her hospital room on most of her last days. Those lines of humanity were made up of soldiers whose hearts she had once touched. They waited as long as it took to give back the simplest gift that had ever been given to them, a warm and gentle hug. (Brooks, 2016 and Stump, 2015)

The Hug Lady, Elizabeth Laird
Jan 15th 1932 - Dec. 24th 2015

AFTER MY departure hug from the Hug Lady, we were finally on our way to the Middle East in early 2004.

THE KUWAITI OVEN & ADIRONDACK BEEF WELLINGTON

The following paragraphs are excerpts from a Congressional Research Service report titled "Kuwait: Governance, Security and U.S. Policy", November 2017, where Middle Eastern affairs specialist Kenneth Katzman gives a brief history of the modern relationship between Kuwait and the United States. The U.S. has been conducting operations in Kuwait since 1991 when Operation Desert Storm ousted Saddam Hussein's invasion and occupation of Kuwait.

U.S.-led coalition forces of nearly 500,000 expelled Iraqi forces from Kuwait in "Operation Desert Storm" (January 16, 1991-February 28, 1991). Kuwait's leaders, who spent the occupation period in Saudi Arabia, were restored to power. Kuwait paid $16.059 billion to offset the U.S. incremental costs of Desert Shield/Desert Storm. After the 1991 war, (until March 2003) about 4,000 U.S. military personnel were stationed at Kuwaiti facilities to conduct containment operations.

Kuwait supported the George W. Bush Administration's decision to militarily overthrow Saddam Hussein (Operation Iraqi Freedom) by hosting the bulk of the U.S. invasion force of about 250,000 forces, in March 2003. Kuwait closed off its entire northern half for weeks before the invasion and provided $266 million to support the combat.

During 2003-2011, an average of 25,000 U.S. troops were based in Kuwait, not including those rotating into Iraq at a given time. Kuwait was the key gateway for U.S. troops entering and exiting Iraq. (Katzman 2017)

After twenty plus hours of flight time, we landed in Kuwait just prior to Valentine's Day in 2004. It's really hot in Kuwait. In fact, the sun in Kuwait will kill you. To state that it's hot in Kuwait is not even close to describing the pain that comes from the sky in the form of burning light.

The sun in Kuwait will kill you. Departing the plane and entering the Kuwaiti atmosphere felt like walking into an oven. Imagine opening the oven on Thanksgiving Day, and then getting inside and curling up next to the turkey. Anything in the suns direct rays had the possibility to burn a finger like a preheated oven rack. The split second experience of stroking your eyebrows to ensure they are still there after looking in the oven too quickly at the roasting turkey, is the only thing that I know of that compares to Kuwait. Except in Kuwait, it's not just a split second flash. Torturous heat was a constant companion to mandatory EyePro.

The sun in Kuwait will kill you. Humans are not intended to or equipped to live and survive on that area of the Earth, although they do. A mid-summer breeze actually made the heat worse because then the heat was in motion. This kept the feeling of possibly melting constantly on your skin. Air was just oxygenated heat that circulated burning pain.

On the bright side, as a "thank you" for saving Kuwaiti independence from Saddam Hussein, U.S. military operations in Kuwait have remained rent free since Operation Desert Storm. In fact, the Kuwaiti government currently subsidizes the U.S. military to remain in their country. Welcome to rent free hell, doubling as a way for the U.S. military to offset some of its costs to wage the Global War on Terror.

The sun in Kuwait will kill you.

Our equipment had not yet arrived at the port in Kuwait. So we had to wait… and wait… and wait. Idle hands are the devils playground. Mercy, we were so bored, and so hot.

Jennifer, soldiers and prisoners are the most innovative people on the face of the planet when it comes to simple forms of entertainment. Sometimes all we have is time.

While we waited we improvised, and did what we could to keep ourselves entertained while trying to stay indoors during the peak heat hours of 0800 – 1800. We occupied our time in hell by building picnic tables and other furniture. We scavenged for scrap lumber and tools, and I actually became quite good at constructing Adirondack chairs out of pallet slats.

While in Kuwait I was commissioned to make an Adirondack chair for First Sergeant (1SG) Bolster. 1SG was a hillbilly who could cause mass bewilderment. His mind was first rate, but he spoke in authentic frontier gibberish. I gained loads of respect for 1SG through our time together. But he sounded like frontier man Gabby Johnston from the movie "Blazing Saddles". 1SG had distinct trouble pronouncing W's and R's. Forget about combining the two letters.

During roll call, Bravo company members had to pay special attention to where 1SG was in the order of the alphabet or they'd miss their name being called. If a name was missed, he would call it out again and without an elbow from a neighbor in formation it was sometimes impossible to understand his incoherent speech. I felt lucky that my last name began with a C, because I only had to listen for a minute. By the time he got to the W's most of us were completely lost. Ward, Wareham, Warren, Wellington, Wilson. I heard the procession of names so many times, I had the order memorized.

When 1SG called out "Wellington", it sounded like a jumbled mess of vowels. Somewhere in the mix was an L, maybe an R, and a T, never in correct order of placement. He simply could not pronounce Wellington. One morning during roll call in the middle of the W's, Wellington forever became known as "Beef".

"Waad," (Ward) yelled Bolster. "Here First Sergeant," was heard in reply.

"Rrrrr-Ham!" (Wareham) "Here First Sergeant."

"Waaarrrnn!" (Warren) "Here First Sergeant."

"Beef," yelled First Sergeant Bolster. No answer. There were looks of bewilderment from everyone who was still actually listening. Did he just say Beef?

"Wilerln-Town!" (Wellington) "Here First Sergeant," replied the confused Wellington.

"BEEF! God-Damn-It! Wreiroln-Town, ya' name's now Beef! Ya' got it son? BEEF!" Bolster explained himself while smiling at the snickers coming from the formation.

"Yes First Sergeant, I got it," replied Beef sheepishly. Kenny Wellington no longer existed. His real name disappeared permanently, and from this moment forward he was referred to as "Beef".

"Wrrrson!" (Wilson) "Here First Sergeant," Wilson replied laughing. The list went on.

1SG gave me $20 dollars for a custom Adirondack chair that a friend and I constructed out of pallet slats.

"Tank you, Srrrgent Caapple," he said handing over the bill.

"My pleasure 1SG. My pleasure."

Adirondack chairs built with love.

AFTER spending a couple months with these men, I began to understand that the bonds we were forming were creating mutual respect for each other, and more than a few lifelong friendships. The next few letters are about some of these people.

I love you Jennifer! I had to throw that in here at least once.

SHENANIGANS

"Vidal Saloon" was the resident barber throughout our entire deployment. Vidal was 43 years of age, although he appeared at first sight to be late-fifties. The pack and a half of Marlboro Reds he smoked every day had wrinkled and stained his face. Years of straight bourbon whiskey had also slightly pickled him. He was 5 foot 2" with an enormous tobacco stained wooly bear caterpillar moustache that completely concealed his upper lip. He had large bushy eyebrows that were replicas of his mustache below. He had a south-east Ohio/West Virginia accent, as did most of the Portsmouth-ians. He looked like a rodent with a rotund pot belly if that is humanly possible.

Vidal brought along a pair of barbershop clippers wherever he went. He was poor, and would cut hair for extra money on Guard Drill weekends back in Portsmouth. I cannot tell you how many times Vidal took $5.00 for cutting someone's hair, and left a quarter inch stripe of hair in an inconspicuous place. The stripe was always something he could "fix" after the unsuspecting victim noticed. That's entertainment innovation right there.

Many of the Soldiers I was with were poor, including me. But there were a few that were log shack next to a stream, dirt floor, no electricity, eat squirrel, trap and sell pelts, poop in a bucket, and cut peoples hair for cigarette money entrepreneur poor. I was fairly certain the paychecks some were currently receiving were the best of their entire lives. They were definitely the best paychecks I had received in my lifetime, to date.

Jen, when considering these circumstances, I think stating that these few individuals were monetarily "poor" is probably a poor choice of words. "Choice of lifestyle" is a more apt description of the few who lived like that. Ease can be found in simplicity, which is a lesson that 99% of Americans could use, myself included.

Our deployment occurred at about the same time the Portsmouth, Ohio area had been inundated with pain clinic pill factory doctors. These doctors would prescribe endless Oxycodone and Percocet to street peddlers for a monetary cut of the profits. The prescription writing drug dealers made national news, and devastated countless lives. The steel plant, the main employer in Portsmouth, had also recently shut its doors. This caused unemployment rates that the area had not seen in decades. There were very few good paying jobs, and these military men, being proud of their roots and their ability to survive, would not walk eagerly into the unemployment or welfare office. At least not the ones I knew. Staying in the Guard brought a guaranteed monthly paycheck of 2-3 hundred dollars. Many of these men needed the National Guard and this deployment. It gave them a means to support their families, and also something to be proud of. So they deployed willingly, as did I!

1SG Bolster employed a dozen or so of the unit members at his family's quarry business. He upped these numbers to nearly 25 after the steel plant closed. Guys said he created jobs in order to keep a small but steady paycheck coming their way. Five men took small pay cuts, so another could have a paycheck. It was this type of act that made these otherwise ordinary men, great men. All of them pulled together to keep their community afloat.

Jennifer, my own father showed me by example many acts of kindness like this when he was managing our hometown hardware and lumber store. It's these types of significant sacrifices that turn an ordinary man into a great man.

A handful of these guys were way past the normal "I believe it is time for me to get out of the Army" date. They were old soldiers. Not that age is the ultimate disqualifier, but it is certainly a factor.

Jennifer, I'm an old soldier now. I feel like I may have a few years left in me, but possibly my own "get out of the Army" date has come.

Somehow, these old men were more proficient at being "Army" than anyone I have come across recently. America hadn't spoiled the lot of them yet. They were rugged, handy, calloused, and knowledgeable. Maybe they were too quick on the draw for a fist fight, but they wouldn't ever imagine pulling a gun. They were helpful, gritty, good natured and well-mannered when need be. They were men who behaved like men. And they were made by similar men before them.

The Army fixed us all up with M16 rifles, the standard issue weapon of the time. These weapons and 120 rounds of ammunition would be our constant companions, along with our EyePro, over the next twelve months.

As an above average marksman myself, I have always felt confident on the rifle range. One of my favorite things to do in the military is to teach a soldier who can't shoot well, how to shoot well. My track record is around 95% success. The Portsmouth guys, all being avid hunters and varmint killers, were on top of their marksmanship game. They didn't need me or the Army to show them how to shoot.

Those who needed them were issued two pairs of prescription EyePro glasses. These glasses were obtained by request during the three physicals and multiple medical examinations with vaccinations etc. that were required for deployment. Standard issue military EyePro prescription glasses of the time were referred to as BCG's, or Birth Control Glasses. They were so awkward looking that they actually worked as a deterrent to the opposite sex.

The shatterproof glass in the BCG's may have been extra thick, but they were effective. Evidently they were even effective through a haze of Marlboro Red cigarette smoke. Vidal could knock the head out of a nickel at fifty yards with his M16, without optics. Only the elite Special Forces soldiers had any scope or optics issued to them back then. Vidal was truly an amazing shot, possibly the best I have ever witnessed. But he was blind as a damn bat without his glasses. This made me wonder if as the resident barber, he left the stripe of hair on purpose or if he truly just couldn't see what he was doing? He couldn't find his Marlboro's if he didn't have his glasses on, and I could have tripped over three packs while walking past him. He had smokes and toothpicks falling out of his pockets.

Vidal told many tall tales about how back home he would go hunting with a slingshot. He hunted and ate squirrel, rabbit, and dove with his "sling" down home. In one particular story about sharpshooting a dove at 35 maybe 40 yards with a ball bearing was so farfetched, that most of us just laughed along with him. Every single story Vidal manufactured had a humorous twist, and we regarded his white lies as we would any standard fish story told among men. Sitting in the evening hours listening to guys like Vidal, Boggs, PawPaw, Nobel and a few others tell their stories was both entertaining and rewarding. Their lives were passed on through spoken word and by example. They were all great story tellers.

E-mail and the internet were becoming fairly conventional for human communication, but hadn't reached the lot of the Portsmouth-ians yet. A few of these guys had never even been on the internet. They were certainly old fashioned and I enjoyed the simplicity that their lifestyle brought along with it. Because he had never ordered anything online before, Boggs asked me to order a sling-shot for Vidal's birthday from Amazon.com.

Wait time for mail while overseas was typically 20-25 days after purchase, and Vidal's slingshot finally arrived. He was overjoyed with his gift. I have never seen a more incredible display of old fashioned marksmanship skills in my entire life, than from that hillbilly and his slingshot. The kill shots Vidal pulled off on plastic Gatorade bottles with randomly selected stones as ammunition and his new rubber band were mind boggling. If I had not witnessed his marksmanship myself, I would have never believed it.

This exhibition brought to light a new respect for Vidal. More importantly, it warranted a new respect for nearly the entire lot of guys from Portsmouth. They truly were a "Band of Brothers". And I was now one of them.

BOZWELL'S TEETH

BOZWELL rounded out Bravo Company 216th Engineers as the oldest deployed engineer in the United States Army. Specialist (his rank) Bozwell was 59 years of age. He actually had to request an age waiver to deploy with us because he would be turning 60 while we were deployed. Age 60 is the mandatory military retirement age. He was from Norwalk and a fellow transfer to the Portsmouth unit. But he had actually grown up in Ironton, Ohio, which is just around the bend from Portsmouth.

Bozwell had made the rank of Staff Sergeant two different times during his career. He had also had that rank taken away two different times. Let's just say that Boz was a little crass around the edges. He was not interested in the politics of the military or anyone's opinions. He was not interested in any Commanding Officer's orders or military compliance whatsoever. Boz and his blundering antics would not stand a chance in the Army today. He was one of the few that kept on showing up for forty years, just for something to do. He was quite set in his careless ways.

The trip to Iraq more than likely prolonged Bozwell's time on earth because he was forced to improve himself physically. And the entire country of Iraq would actually run out of cigarettes periodically, forcing him to do without. That may have been the reason the crazy old coot decided he wanted to go with us. Or maybe it was just something to do?

One morning we were all called to formation prior to heading off in separate directions to accomplish our daily tasks. We soon learned the reason for the formation. We were going to take a platoon photo to send back home to our families. We were in the Kuwaiti desert now, and had new desert colored uniforms, so why not snap a few photos?

When Boz became privy to the purpose for the formation, he exclaimed loudly, "A picture? We're takin' a picture? Hol' on jus'a minute ya' rascals. Le'me go git' ma' teeth."

B. Company 216th Engineer Battalion (minus a few).

THE CAT IS OUT OF THE BAG

THE TOC (Tactical Operations Center) in Kuwait was the tent where all decisions that mattered were made. The 1st Infantry Division (ID) ran the TOC with a welcome to rent free hell committee for all units that would fall underneath the 1st ID in Iraq. That included us as the engineers. The Commanding Officer of the welcoming committee was Lieutenant Colonel (LTC) Aker, from Alabama… Roll Tide. He was instantly a friendly foe for those of us who were Ohio State Buckeye football fans.

The Army rank of LTC is a silver oak leaf. From afar it looks like a circle or an "egg". The next rank higher is Colonel (COL) and is represented by a rigid looking eagle. It is said that once a person makes the rank of COL, the egg hatches and they sprout their wings. LTC Aker would soon sprout his wings, and deservedly so.

Aker was a man of few unnecessary words. He never smiled and took his mission very seriously. He had the reverse of what I would normally call dimples. Due to his lack of emotion no one ever saw the white of his teeth underneath his jowls.

A friend of mine, Clark, was just the opposite in nature, and was constantly smiling. He and I combined our humorous forces and came up with the acronym CAT, for "Colonel Aker's Teeth". Neither of us had ever had the great privilege of witnessing CAT. I honestly assumed the guy had dentures that he never wore.

Within a week we would head north, as our equipment had finally arrived. We had been in Kuwait just shy of a month, and had gotten into the rhythm of sitting through LTC Aker's Current Operations in Iraq briefing, three times a week. It was the only conduit we had for information on the current situation in the theater of operations we were about to enter. Clark and I sat in on one of the final briefings we would witness from LTC Aker. During the updated synopsis of operations in Iraq, LTC Aker gave an extraordinarily large, unprecedented smile. He had teeth!

Clark, without hesitation and very pleased with himself, let out a much louder than normal whisper. "The CAT is out of the bag." I lost my composure immediately and laughed uncontrollably, interrupting LTC Aker's briefing.

CAT had no doubt heard my outburst and momentarily stopped his briefing. He searched the small audience, looking for the disrespectful interrupter. I quickly zipped my lips to adhere to the required respect and compliance.

Not missing a beat, Clark leaned over and wittily whispered in my direction, "The CAT got your tongue?" I had to excuse myself. Clark followed my lead seconds after I left the tent.

The time had come for us to head north. It was time to head into the real war in Iraq. We had built Adirondack chairs, cut each other's hair, and had seen the "CAT". However, we had yet to cross paths with the black cat.

V

Learning to Run

"On the Run" by The Jompson Brothers (Featuring Chris Stapleton) from the album "The Jompson Brothers", 2010.

https://www.youtube.com/watch?v=VEjgsMKYOUo

The wind is blowin' cold and dark
On the road with no way out
Chained to all the things I've done
On the run
I wear misery like a veil
And I don't get much sleep
Of broken hearts and smokin' gun
On the run

I've been runnin' from the day, runnin' from the night
Washin' my hands on the bloody riverside
Runnin' from the truth, runnin' from a lie
Tryin' to get away, but I just can't hide

Guilty conscience slows me down
I'm the only friend I've got
So I keep whiskey on my tongue
On the run

I've been runnin' from the day, runnin' from the night
Washin' my hands on the bloody riverside
Runnin' from the truth, runnin' from a lie
Tryin' to get away, but I just can't hide
On the run

IT WAS TIME to officially enter the war. Jennifer, everything you have read up to this point has been sort of an introduction to the real story I set out to tell. The desire to continue with stories of Adirondack chairs and Good Idea Fairies is certainly pleasing. And although there are many more stories like them, it is time to switch gears and begin the journey down the rocky path to where the skeletons reside.

INTO IRAQ WITH PAWPAW

In Bravo Company, there was a single Vietnam War veteran among our ranks. He was affectionately known as "Pawpaw", and was one of the very few people in our unit that could proudly wear a combat patch on the right sleeve of his uniform. A combat patch is something earned after performing duty in a designated combat zone. There were very few combat patches on military uniforms at the time, because prior to 9/11/2001, the last large scale combat operation was the six week long Operation Desert Storm, in 1991.

Pawpaw and I were placed on a lead team of individuals who would move on to Forward Operating Base (FOB) Speicher near Tikrit, Iraq, prior to the rest of the Battalion's arrival. Where we would obtain living quarters and scope out the requirements of the FOB. We would be the representatives from Bravo Company.

Crossing the border into Iraq from Kuwait would be a big deal for everyone. We would be entering a real combat zone, and would forever be afforded the honor of wearing a combat patch on the right shoulder of our uniforms, just like Pawpaw. We would no longer be "slick sleeve" soldiers.

The following excerpts are from a Congressional Research Service report titled "Iraq: Politics and Governance", March, 2016.

> *The territory that is now Iraq fell under the rule of the Ottoman Empire in the 16th Century. Ottoman rule lasted until World War I, in which that empire was defeated and its dominions in the*

Middle East were taken over by the European powers that had defeated the Ottomans in the war. Britain took over Iraq (then still called "Mesopotamia"). Iraq gained independence in 1932.

Saddam Hussein came to power in Iraq (in 1979) about six months after Ayatollah Ruhollah Khomeini's Islamic revolution ousted the U.S.-backed Shah in neighboring Iran. Saddam apparently perceived Iran's revolution as an existential threat with a potential to inspire a Shiite-led revolution in Iraq, which is about 60% Shiite Arab, 20% Sunni Arab, and 18% Kurdish.

A U.S.-led military coalition that included about 250,000 U.S. troops crossed the border from Kuwait into Iraq on March 19, 2003, to oust the regime of Saddam Hussein and eliminate suspected remaining WMD programs. After several weeks of combat, the regime of Saddam Hussein fell on April 9, 2003. During the 2003-2011 presence of U.S. forces, Iraq completed a transition from that dictatorship to a plural political system in which varying sects and ideological and political factions compete in elections. (Katzman and Humud, 2016)

Almost one year after the first Global War on Terror troops crossed the Kuwaiti border into Iraq, I hopped on a C-130 airplane and strapped into the cargo net seating for a short flight to FOB Anaconda, at 2:00 AM local time. Anaconda was just outside the city of Balad, Iraq, and north of Bagdad by about 50 miles.

Pawpaw, on the other hand, gingerly stepped on board the plane. He was weighted heavily with the burden of all the required combat gear he was wearing. A full combat load of ammunition and protective gear is around eighty extra lbs. for an average size person to carry. The weight of that equipment wore me out and I was young and in exceptionally good physical shape. Pawpaw was by no means in bad shape... his nickname was Pawpaw. You can make the obvious connection.

I have ridden some mean rollercoasters and would not shy away from any thrill ride on the face of the planet. I have rappelled from 200 foot towers into windows, completed a couple Australian style rappels by jumping face first down the side of a building, and have hurled myself off every high dive and cliff into whatever water was below, at every opportunity. I once did a backflip off a thirty foot bridge into six feet of water, just for the thrill. And out of all those extremes, nothing, I mean absolutely nothing, compares to combat dropping out of the sky and landing in a combat zone.

Before taking off in Kuwait we were warned that landing the C-130 could sometimes be a little bit hairy. Forty minutes into the flight a crewmember motioned for us to strap into the cargo netting seats. We were all wearing headsets for communication purposes and he stated that he would cut off our internal communications so the pilots could communicate effectively with the ground tower during our landing. We were then told to put on our protective Kevlar helmets. I thought that that was a great idea! Let the pilots do their job and land this plane!

Our internal radio silence began, and the pilot in control immediately dove for the ground. Unrepaired holes in the aircraft's hull created an incessant cobra hiss when we started our speeding decent. It's a good thing we were strapped in because I'm certain I would have ended up on the ceiling. During some impromptu movements of that speedy decent, I honestly didn't know which way was up anymore. The forces that the pilot put on that plane caused moments of weightlessness. It felt like I was inside an Olympic ten meter high dive competition vessel. We seemed to do a triple twisting, double inverted flip, and even bent in half into the pike position at one point. I knew we were going down, but had no idea of velocity, impact, or distance. I was terrified.

Then the M61 Vulcans mounted on the exterior of that propeller driven aircraft, nicknamed the flying brick, gave off a few long bursts, followed by a few more. M61's are six-barrel, air-cooled, Gatling style rotary cannons that fire 20mm (millimeter) rounds at 1000's of rounds per minute. Hearing those guns go off just outside the wall of the C-130 flying brick airship put things immediately into perspective.

We were either returning fire because we were being fired upon, or we were laying down suppressive fire. At that moment it hit me for the first time. I sure as hell wasn't in Ohio anymore.

During my first jittery step off that C-130 onto Iraqi soil my fingertips were blue due to the clenched grip I had just had around the cargo netting inside the plane.

"Welcome to Iraq, Sergeant", from a smirking jaw were the first words spoken to me as Pawpaw and I were rushed off the tarmac.

Sergeant Smith was dirty, unshaven, and his protective gear was torn and tattered. The first guy I met in Iraq was named Smith. I will remember his name forever. The fabric camouflage cover on his Kevlar helmet had a rip large enough to expose over half of the bare helmet. The torn fabric partially draped over his forehead. The Iraqi atmosphere smelled of automotive grease, gasoline, and landfill. There were whiffs of roadkill about every fifth breath. I shook his dirty hand and took particular notice of his sunken eyes. He looked as if he hadn't slept in weeks. He offered us a smoke break before we'd get on the road north, to Tikrit. Pawpaw and I declined, but Smith took the break anyway. He motioned for us to follow him, as he lit up a Camel full flavor cigarette.

"What in the hell is that smell?" Pawpaw asked of him.

"You'll get used to it. The entire country smells like this," was his intolerant answer.

Conversation was kept to bare minimum. It was as if Smith wasn't even there. He was not focused on anything except the long soothing draws from his cigarette.

Not another word was spoken. Radio silence...

I distinctly remember riding in the back of a dump truck at first light on the same morning we landed in Iraq. We were on Main Supply Route (MSR) Tampa on our way to Forward Operating Base (FOB) Speicher near Tikrit. Our personal M16 weapons were locked and loaded. Drive fast and don't stop was/is the best defense to avoid Improvised Explosive Devices (IED's), the war's most lethal killer. So, we sped up over the course of a couple minutes to the top speed of 50 mph in the massively heavy cargo truck. The desire for more speed and maneuverability was futile.

Pawpaw was sitting directly across from me all the way to the rear of the truck bed. We hit a large pot hole that shot him a couple feet into the air and he slammed back down onto the steel cargo bed seating.

He winced in pain and muttered, "What the hell am I doing here?" He was never quite the same after that.

The ride into country and a pothole had literally squashed Pawpaw's second round of wartime aspirations. It was quite difficult watching him go through the realization that he was not the young whipper snapper of old. He had wanted to go out and fight for his country once again. But he could barely walk. That pothole had rendered him ineffective. Although what he really needed was to go home to "fort living room", a couch, a heavy dosage of Advil, and some of his wife's homemade chicken noodle soup, he wasn't about to give up.

After a few very rough months of hobbling around on FOB Speicher, Pawpaw ended up being sent home unwillingly. He was a tough old bull.

> *The true soldier fights not because he hates what is in front of him, but because he loves what is behind him.*
>
> - G.K. Chesterton

ONE WEEK LATER our entire Battalion finally arrived in Iraq. We combined forces with a "sister" battalion of Combat Engineers from North Dakota, who married up with us Construction Engineers from Ohio for missions. Just like you and your sister, Jennifer, we too were a force to be reckoned with.

ENGINEER MISSION & TACTICS

During our first month in Iraq, the North Dakota Combat Engineers, who had arrived several months prior to us, were literally writing the book on the relatively new concept of route clearance. Although they have been refined, parts of their original military doctrine on route clearance are still used at Explosives Ordinance Disposal (EOD) School.

Route clearance is the deliberate search for and destroying of IED's. It has proven itself to be the most dangerous mission throughout the entire war.

Alongside the N.D. Guard, supporting them and nearly everything and everyone else under the 1st Infantry Division's command, were the 216th Engineers. We Ohioans with all our heavy equipment were a hot commodity within the area of operations. We made soldiers safe by "digging" them in. We cleared areas, pushed up earthen berms and built structures for the rest of the coalition forces to occupy. Everyone loved to see us. We brought safety and creature comforts along with us.

There had never been a mission in the history of the military like the one the North Dakota Guardsmen were undertaking. There have been countless since, but they were the first. These men were deliberately looking for roadside bombs (IED's), and that was crazy to begin with. They were also driving slowly in canvas sided vehicles, just waiting for these IED's to explode on them, which was double crazy. The cherry to top it all off was that if they found an IED that had not detonated, they were required to detonate it. They would actually shoot a couple rounds at it, from a distance, in hopes of detonation. If the IED didn't explode, they would have to walk out to the IED and hand place secondary explosives on it, for a controlled detonation. Triple insanity.

The term "controlled detonation" when referring to an IED, must be used loosely. A soldier had no "control" over a cell phone call. A call which was being made to a phone that was attached to a 155mm artillery round's ignitor (155mm rounds were the most common IED). A soldier had no control over an oven timer. Oven timers were being recycled for jihad, strapped to an IED's ignitor, and set to go off in three hours. Happy Thanksgiving, your turkey is cooked.

A soldier had no control over Al-Qaeda's original IED detonation intent. Soldiers just hoped to God that they had control over how an IED was going to detonate.

When on a mission that requires deliberately looking for bombs, one does not typically ride a bicycle. The canvas sided hummers that N.D. Guardsmen were using for route clearance had little more blast protection than a ten speed bike. In a partial solution to the lack of blast protection, we cut plates of steel and diamond plate cargo truck lining with plasma torches. These plates were hung on the outsides of their vehicles in an attempt at some blast protection. Their vehicles looked like a bunch of trucks from the movie "Mad Max", rolling down the highway.

The controversial question at the time, asked directly to then Secretary of Defense Donald Rumsfeld, was: why were under equipped American soldiers getting blown up in unarmored canvas vehicles? I am certain both the North Dakota and Ohio National Guard families wrote those letters to their congressmen.

Rumsfeld's reply was, "You go to war with the Army you have." He was right, and we did.

Canvas top hummer modified with ¼ inch steel sheathing for gunner protection.

One of my Battalion's missions was to follow the Infantry and "dig in". After they occupied an area, we would soon follow in a long convoy of slow moving construction and earth moving equipment. Slow is smooth and smooth is fast. It was strange to roll up into a completely open swath of land alongside a paved road with tanks placed at the corners. You could normally see them for miles. There was little to no protection out there. In the flat desert wasteland, the Iraqi people and the undifferentiated Al-Qaeda terrorists would just drive right on by. When we finally arrived alongside the infantry we were generally safe and we were utilized as expected, running our equipment and digging in.

During our year in Iraq the coalition force tripled in size, and we were utilized every single day in some facet, to make safe places for new soldiers to live. We were very busy, very efficient and had quickly mastered our craft. Our services were needed by everyone. With my construction background, I very quickly became a go-to guy for answers to many questions. And I had good answers.

In the beginning, I was scared out of my gourd every time we went somewhere new, which was a frequent occurrence. IED's were the ultimate equalizer at the time and everyone was scared of them and their unpredictability. At least I wasn't looking for the IED's, though.

If I had deployed in my original capacity as a Combat Engineer, I would have been performing the route clearance mission. If I wasn't with the Construction Engineers from Portsmouth, Ohio, I'd have been carrying out the same mission as the North Dakota (N.D.) engineers.

A short aside: None of us knew it in early 2004, but my home unit, Charlie Company, 612th Combat Engineer Battalion, from Norwalk, Ohio would be performing the route clearance mission in Bagdad by early 2005. In an interesting moment, my home unit buddies passed me by, on their way into Iraq. On the other side of the highway, I was on my way out of Iraq with my new war torn buddies from Portsmouth. Yes, that actually happened.

The Norwalk unit had some new armored hummers with built in protective machine gun turrets, a few Mine Resistant Ambush Protected (MRAP) armored vehicles, and upgraded body armor. I was happy that they would enter the country better equipped than we had.

Unfortunately that was still not enough. Army Specialist, Jeremy M. Hodge, of Ridgeway, Ohio, while assigned to Bravo Company, 612th Combat Engineer Battalion, was KIA on October 10, 2005. You will never be forgotten.

Within the initial 2-3 months of 2004, my battalion incurred a few combat injuries garnering Purple Hearts, but no one was severely wounded. The North Dakota Guardsmen were much less fortunate. Four men were KIA, and five or six more severely wounded soldiers were sent home. March/April 2004 were the deadliest months to date for coalition forces in the War on Terror. I am uncertain if that statistic still stands today, but I would not be surprised if it did. The entire country of Iraq felt the squeeze of the war claw in early 2004.

The North Dakota unit was getting rid of the enemy's number one threat to all of us by destroying IED's. Therefore the N.D. guys were number one on the enemy hit list. They were taking a majority of all the confrontation in our area, and they were wearing thin in their already thin vehicles.

Meanwhile, Mechanized Infantry rolled around Iraq in their M1 tanks day after day, relatively unharmed.

The infantry's tanks were much like a herd of elephants to the insufficiently armed Al-Qaeda. A rational person does not poke a bull elephant in the ear with a sharpened stick. Not this guy, and not any relatively smart terrorist either. There were much softer targets to poke, like the Ohio, and especially the North Dakota units. Both of our battalions were being attacked at relatively high percentages.

Post deployment, a 216th Engineer staff officer crunched the numbers for the entire Battalion's year of missions. With his analysis, he found that nearly 15% of the time that we rolled out of any FOB gates and onto Iraqi streets, an IED went off or we ended up in some sort of skirmish. One out of every seven are pretty good odds for Texas Hold'em poker players, but not when it's your life on the line.

A PEACEFUL DAY, turned violent. On Easter Sunday 2004, I awoke to my alarm clock at 4:00 AM, for a 4:30 sunrise church service. It was one of the most beautiful sights I have ever witnessed. About 150 metal chairs were set up in the middle of the desert, facing the sunrise, while the war boomed on directly behind us. The sun actually sparkled off the sand in its early acute angles to the earth, before it rose above and relentlessly beat the hard desert scape.

With memories like this one, it's true that two people in the exact same place, at the exact same time, can have very different recollections of how things happened. It happened so fast and I have heard the stories told so many times over the years that some of the details of the incident are pretty fuzzy. Jennifer, this is how I remember Easter Sunday, 2004.

EASTER ADRENALINE

After Easter sunrise service, some members of the 216th and I were headed out on a mission that none of us were too excited about. I cannot explain it, but somehow we just had this feeling things were about to get rough. The insurgency had taken over Fallujah, but we were unaware of the 6-8 months of turmoil that was about to ensue in the Iraqi city. It was not yet part of history but was history in the making right before our very own eyes.

> *Operation Vigilant Resolve had kicked off in the city of Fallujah, Iraq. The operation had begun because of the killing and mutilation of four private military contractors on March 31, 2004, and five American soldiers a few days prior. Abu Musab al-Zarqawi was originally suspected as the organizer of the ambush as he was known to planning terror attacks and believed to be in the area. (First Battle of Fallujah, n.d.)*

Within the 216th Battalion, we had two convoys on separate missions that day. Both of our convoys were headed to destinations in the same vicinity. That morning, unbeknownst to us, the N.D. Guard lost two men who were KIA in an IED explosion. This happened right outside of Fallujah. My convoy was not too far behind them.

We were on a mission to dig a few temporary fighting positions for a group of Marines, who would be spending an unknown amount of time in Fallujah. As a gunner in the convoy, I rode in the back of a five ton dump truck down Main Supply Route (MSR) Tampa from Tikrit. I was armed with a M2 50 caliber (50cal) machine gun. It was mounted on a turret constructed from a piece of four inch metal pipe. A homemade wall of sandbags was piled about waist high around me. Above my belly button, save for the protective vest I was wearing, I was open to the Iraqi atmosphere.

About five miles from our destination and the awaiting Marines, a rocket propelled grenade (RPG) shot towards us and cleared the hood of another truck in our convoy by inches. This was the beginning of an ambush on our small convoy from the right side of the road. Seconds after the RPG exploded into the ground just past our vehicles, AK-47 machine gun fire erupted. Another RPG was fired in at head level. It flew right between my mounted machine gun and the rear of the truck's cab. It shot through a small cube of open air directly in front of me, and exploded fifty feet beyond me on a sand berm. The barrel of the weapon that was in my hands had residue stains from the propellant in that rocket. It was permanently tarnished by the RPG's fuel.

Simultaneously, an IED exploded with a loud concussive wave directly in front of the lead vehicle of our convoy. We believe it was made of two or three, 155mm artillery rounds. There were secondary sounds of shrapnel from the blast flying by, and impacting all around us. The concussion and shockwave was certainly felt by all.

The tactics that this group of Al-Qaeda utilized were quite sound, as we were now basically trapped. We were pinned down, and had to fight our way out of this situation. As an instant reaction to the years of training I had received and the heat of the moment, my thumbs squeezed down on the butterfly trigger of my M2 50cal machine gun. Dirt flung into the air close to where the enemy RPG's had been fired, as the powerful thump-thump-thump of my massive weapon sang.

I quickly adjusted my sight picture upwards by a few feet on target, aimed and fired again. A pink mist erupted behind one of the armed silhouettes I had fired upon. The ejected round casings made a pinging sound of metal on metal as they dropped quickly, but individually into the bed of the dump truck. The blood of my enemy had entered the air. I had seen the pink mist. The human silhouette that was full of the same fears I was a moment ago, had exploded. A couple of 50cal rounds will rip a body into pieces.

This was the first confirmed kill that I had during my deployment. There were others that I would bet the ranch on, and some that were very good possibilities. This one was different because it was the first. The death of this man was undeniably a direct result of my pulling the trigger.

I had trained for incidents such as this one for years. However, this firefight was real, and confirming the death of an enemy changes a man. Confirmation of another man attempting to take your life also changes a man. The sight of the pink mist is now permanently ingrained as a violent memory inside my head.

After the first RPG missed all of us, one of the truck drivers in our convoy accidentally sat on the key to his radio's microphone. This allowed everyone in our convoy to hear him belt out Metallica's "Enter Sandman" during the entire firefight. He had a battery powered radio, which was playing a Metallica CD inside his truck. He carried a great tune right along with James Hetfield (Metallica's lead singer), never missing a beat, through all the bullets and explosions. He serenaded us with Metallica during the entire firefight, while not even knowing he was doing so.

The driver in the lead vehicle of our convoy would never hear the same out of his right ear again. He was closest to the IED blast. A piece of shrapnel from the IED, roughly the size of my palm, was lodged in a sandbag inches from my left kidney.

Luckily for all of us, Al-Qaeda's aim was off by inches and their IED timing was off by a split second. The smoke finally cleared from the ambush and we ended up on a small FOB outside of Fallujah. We stayed that night in a small tent, and shared watch duty with the other residents of the FOB.

Firepower superiority, dead terrorists, a few minor injuries, and some damaged vehicles. Embracing the suck of the moment that had just unfolded, we celebrated our "good times" and our victory. We were all obviously happy about not being severely injured, or dying.

Personally, I did not properly distinguish or separate the aspects of not dying, and killing another man. The incidents were one in the same to me. Not making the distinction, I was happy about both.

> Jennifer, we spent the next couple of nights on that small FOB with little communication to the rest of the world. We filled the time by telling each other our own versions of the ambush incident over, and over, and over, and over again. I had reoccurring dreams of the pink mist almost immediately. I would not call them nightmares until much later in life, as they had little effect on my demeanor for the remainder of my Iraq deployment.

After that Easter Sunday, I stayed in various other lovely accommodations in and around Fallujah. I repeatedly assisted with bringing equipment and supplies to the area. It seemed like every time Fallujah was involved, we were in some sort of skirmish. I would lock all of these memories, and those of the pink mist, deep inside the catacombs of my mind. And I would be unwilling to revisit them for many, many years.

Not another word was spoken. Radio silence…

THIS LETTER briefly steps out of the chronology, but it also occurred in the city of Fallujah. That city was a nightmare, Jennifer. That city is where some of my nightmares live.

BLOOD FACE – ANOTHER FALLUJAH STORY

Just prior to Thanksgiving, 2004, I was in Fallujah with a team of 4-5 other engineers. We arrived at our destination the evening prior, and had just missed the bulk of a ground battle that had ensued over the 48 hours prior. We drove onto the compound of U.S. Marines, with just enough light to integrate ourselves into the small encampment for the night.

On arrival, we knew we would be remaining in Fallujah for at least the next 24 hours. Our mission was to dig a few hasty fighting positions for the Marines and their vehicles. We had a couple of dump trucks and a bulldozer on a tractor trailer, with which to execute our mission.

None of us had gotten much sleep after nightfall. Thunderous explosions from targeted airstrikes boomed on throughout the night. The explosions were like a late summer storm which lit up the sky for a brief second, before retreating into the darkness. Yet they were unlike any storm from Mother Nature that I had ever witnessed. During many of the explosions, we could feel the ground shake beneath us.

Fallujah was the most dangerous city on the face of the planet, and I was in the middle of it with a bunch of battered yet still war-hungry Marines. That morning, we all stood in the middle of the wreckage of a city which had unwillingly twisted itself into a battlefield. As the eastern sky began to turn pink and orange from the rising sun, some of the Marines were shaving or taking a quick break. They were eating an MRE (prepackaged Meal Ready to Eat) breakfast while the war around them permitted. We engineers were less than 24 hours from our most recent shower and hot meal. There was no telling how long these Marines had been without those amenities.

A Gunnery Sergeant, E-7, Marine, was occupying his peaceful moment that morning by shaving. While he looked at his own reflection in the side mirror attached to his hummer, I watched as he pulled his razor down the side of his face. The shaving cream hit the ground with a puff of dust after each flick of his wrist. It had hints of pink within it. I approached him to informally break the ice and to receive direction from him. He would advise us on the digging mission which the other engineers and I were to accomplish.

I attempted to give him a small package of baby wipes (standard combat uniform pocket cargo), to refresh and clean up with after his shave. He declined my offer while pointing toward the pink shaving cream piles on the ground beneath him.

He then stated hoarsely, "I didn't cut myself. That's not my blood, Sergeant." Those are words that I will never forget.

I replaced the small package of baby wipes into the cargo pocket of my uniform. I was slightly confused by the words he had just spoken. I was just being kind by offering him a solution to clean off his face after shaving.

As he turned toward me, I could see that the entire right side of his torso was covered in blood. Not acknowledging my certain looks of astonishment, he extended his hand and a red stained forearm. I shook his hand and he welcomed me and the other engineers to Fallujah. Small talk was not a part of the conversation. He gave some very brief directions and we began digging immediately.

Not another word was spoken. Radio silence…

I'll never know whose blood the Gunnery Sergeant was removing from his cheek that morning. But by the blank looks in those young men's eyes, they had seen a lot of it. I had been through some shit myself, but was full of sympathy for those men. They would never see the world in the same light as they did prior to Fallujah.

Experiencing moments like this one kept me going full steam ahead during my Iraq deployment, and throughout my entire military career. I could not imagine letting these men down. Therefore, I would not let these men down.

That is the true "Stuff of Legend".

I WAS ABLE to find a few answers to life's questions in the midst of the longest year of my life. Among the questions I am now able to answer is: what did I want to be when I grew up? Jen, what did you want to be when you grew up? My guess is that an accountant wasn't on top of the list.

This fulfilling story is about a couple of remarkable men I once knew, and a great man that I still know. This story is indeed an important part of how I got here.

THE ANSWER TO AN AGE OLD QUESTION

Used to waking up at the crack of dawn, Harry Nobel and Mike Boggs were descendants of many generations of blue collar hard working men. They were two of the most useful men I have ever known. If a job required fixing, building, or constructing, they could do it.

Nobel and Boggs were the exception to the rule when it came to military rank on the jobsite. Normally if someone of higher rank has an idea, that idea wins. If Nobel or Boggs had an idea or they told someone to do something a certain way, it was done that way. They won, discussion over, no questions asked. It was an unwritten rule that if they were in the area they somehow became the boss of the entire operation. They would wander from jobsite to jobsite giving pointers and explaining why we should do things this way rather than the way we were about to do them. Even if it seemed like their idea was absurd at the moment, somehow they always ended up being correct. I learned scores of useful things from both of these knowledgeable men.

Every single morning like clockwork at 0415, even on Nobel's day off, there were aromas of freshly brewed coffee and mild cigarette smoke wafting from his area. If you waited 20 minutes, at about 0435 there was always the smell of bacon mixing in with the coffee and dull smoke. Nobel, being a well-travelled union carpenter, had brought a coffee pot and an electric skillet with him to Iraq. Every bit of electricity utilized was generated by diesel powered generators that droned on at all hours. Regardless, I could always smell and hear the bacon cooking. The sounds and smells reminded me of the iron skillet back home. Many mornings I'd find myself wandering into his room at 0430, where I'd have a small cup of coffee with Nobel before my morning workout.

Boggs was always sharing a couple slices of bacon with Nobel when I returned from my morning run. They'd never miss a day of this morning routine. I wondered what thrilling deal of a trade had taken place in order for them to have obtained daily bacon rations.

While sharing a cup of coffee at 0430 on a morning that I wasn't going to work out, Nobel asked me if I'd like to have some bacon. I would, absolutely! How could I resist the wonderful smell that had wafted into my nose daily for what seemed like months?

Not having any plates, we used the plastic lids of coffee cans. He placed two slices of the lightly browned, cured pork, fresh off the skillet onto a lid and handed it to me. I could not wait to sink my teeth into all the salty goodness of a fresh piece of bacon. I allowed it to cool for thirty seconds and lifted a piece over my mouth, dropping and folding it in its entirety onto my watering tongue.

It was Spam! It was disgusting ground up jellied and formed, bacon flavored meat leftovers that melted into a liquid paste in my mouth. I wanted to barf. I declined any further offers of bacon from Nobel in the mornings, but always enjoyed his company, a cup of coffee, and the smell of the imaginary bacon that sizzled in the background.

Bacon spam and wintergreen flavored Skoal Bandits chewing tobacco were the Mike Boggs version of Popeye's spinach. He was the strongest man on earth. Boggs dined with Nobel each morning on 3-4 slices of fried spam, and when he wasn't eating he had a small pouch of chewing tobacco between his cheek and gum. Not an abnormally large man at about 6'2" and 220-lbs, he still had superhuman strength. I witnessed Boggs do extraordinary things, like carry two 150-lb. hummer tires, one in each hand, on multiple occasions. He was always eager for a wraslin' match but never had any takers. The challenged were too fearful of an impending ass whoopin' to accept.

Boggs had bratwursts for fingers that were attached to his grizzly bear paws. He used his bratwursts to pick and play the mandolin. The strongest man on earth played the smallest guitar on earth quite well. Three or four of the guys would get together once a week and pick and grin. They'd play bluegrass music together and tell stories about everything from weather to women. I thoroughly enjoyed the pickin' and grinnin' sessions, and would even belt out the vocals on a tune with them occasionally.

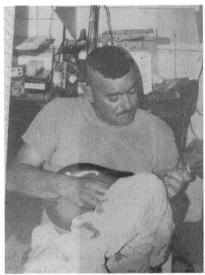

Boggs and his Mandolin

Throughout the entire deployment period, I formed a great appreciation for the simple and hard working lifestyle of these men. They were far removed from the academic naivety and necktie wearing tendencies of my time at Wittenberg University. Don't get me wrong, I loved everything about Wittenberg and the excellent education that it afforded me. Go Tigers! I would not exchange that experience in my life for anything. But it wasn't until I spent some time with a few men from Portsmouth that I knew what my professional life was going to consist of. They taught me that I would find happiness professionally by combining my education with some form of labor intensive skillsets. That type of profession would keep me feeling useful throughout my time on earth. Some smarts and loads of usefulness are humble things that are the keys to a simple man's inner happiness.

I never saw either of these men again after we came home from Iraq. Our lives travelled down drastically different paths. Unfortunately, I heard that Boggs was diagnosed with liver cancer and passed away soon after we returned home from Iraq. I imagine Nobel is still starting his day the exact same way I know he enjoyed by making his bacon each morning with a cup of strong black coffee and a smoke. For the rest of his day I imagine he would be constructing something awesome in his retirement wood shop.

And so, it was through these men I learned the answer to the question that is asked to all children, ages three through thirty: what do you want to be when you grow up? My answer changed from what I always thought it was supposed to be, a profession, to a person.

"My Dad… I want to be my Father when I grow up. The smartest and most useful man I know."

Thanks Dad. Unknowingly, you have been instilling smarts and usefulness into my head since I was born. Thank you. For watching me smack my thumb while pounding and bending countless nails into a 2x4 on the garage floor at four years of age, and challenging me to get three in a row. Then that same evening, insisting that I rewrite my full name with no mistakes. For letting me help you varnish a piece of wood furniture with an old t-shirt, and making me finish my math homework correctly. For teaching me how to change the oil in a car, and to also have an appreciation for the arts. For letting me brown the beef for our Sunday pot of chili, and challenging me to reflect on a book report. Teaching me how to love a woman unconditionally by watching you and Mom is one of the most useful lessons I'll ever learn. The list goes on infinitely.

I set out to write a short story about a couple of great men I knew once upon a time in Iraq, and consequently found that you have been teaching me the key to finding true inner peace and happiness my entire life. The written word led me straight to the greatest man I've ever known. I have found the answer to the question, and that answer has always been right in front of me. Love ya' Pops.

THIS STORY explains how and why some of us Ohio boys became part of the North Dakota Engineer's route clearance mission. It was a huge turning point for the lot of us who were chosen to perform this very important and very demanding mission. Let's go back to Easter Sunday and the pink mist.

ENGINEER MISSION & TACTICS II – TRAILBLAZER

After losing their fifth and sixth men on Easter Sunday, and issuing countless more first class plane tickets directly to Walter Reed Veterans Hospital, the North Dakota Battalion Commander, a Lieutenant Colonel (LTC), made the decision that his unit had endured enough. The day after Easter he approached our Battalion Commander, a Portsmouth local, and asked him for help. His simple plea was a most honorable and lifesaving endeavor.

The two Lieutenant Colonels worked together along with their staff officers, and they thoughtfully devised a plan to transform the existing military doctrine on route clearance into what it is today. They presented the idea to the 1st Infantry Division Commander, who wore two stars on his hat, Major General John Batiste.

Their plan was clear to those of us who were also trained in demolitions. Fellow Combat Engineer cross-levelled soldiers had discussed the same ideas. Their plan consisted of the utilization of heavy earthmoving equipment in combination with demolitions teams for the route clearance mission.

Specialized and protective equipment was "on the way", promised Secretary of Defense Donald Rumsfeld, but, "you go to war with the Army you have."

We were all promised new up-armored vehicles, vehicle kits, and better protection from blasts. But lack of this equipment could not stop the war effort, especially the route clearance mission. It was essential to the entire war to keep the supply routes as safe as possible, and open to our troops at all the various Forward Operating Bases (FOB's) around Iraq.

General Batiste approved the proposal from the two National Guard Engineer Battalion Commander's, and offered the full support of the 1st Infantry Division.

Overnight, we became Task Force Trailblazer. Trailblazer was a multi-unit operation of engineer awesomeness, formed by combining equipment from our Ohio unit with the demolitions expertise of the North Dakota unit.

At the time, we Ohio engineers had some of the best protective equipment in Iraq for the route clearance mission. We had bulldozers and thick walled trucks that were made to push dirt and move tons of earth. The blade of the dozer was 3-5 inches thick and would deflect just about any blast. We had already lined the walls and floors of some of our equipment with sand bags, for our own protection on convoys. We had also welded three inch galvanized steel pipe to a platform and bolted it to the center of a few dump truck beds. Essentially, we had built machine gun firing turrets in vehicles which would now double as mobile IED spotting stations.

Within days, more of our trucks were modified for blast protection with as much quarter inch steel as possible, and sandbags were placed wherever they would stack. This was very similar to what we had done to the N.D. equipment a few months prior. The difference was that our heavy equipment was originally manufactured with much more thick-walled steel, therefore providing more blast protection.

The war wouldn't come to a stop while waiting on new protective equipment, so neither would we.

2.5 ton cargo truck, a "Deuce and a half", modified with plywood supports for sandbags. 50cal machine gun in a makeshift turret.

Brimming with piss and vinegar, and some twenty something naivety, I was young, pre-children, and would have taken on the world if allowed. Many soldiers broke down when they were asked to be a part of this new mission. Raising my hand, I volunteered. After all, I knew what I was doing. Having already been trained as a Combat Engineer, I knew the demolitions aspect of the mission.

The idea of being part of one of the most important missions in the war excited me, but at the same time it also made my heart drop into the sand just a little. During our first few months in Iraq, the route clearance mission had shown itself as the most dangerous, by a landslide. And I was now going to be a part of it.

Jennifer, I live at peace today because of my decisions. I did not fail my country or my fellow Soldier. I can honestly say I did all things possible. I stepped out of all comfort zones by volunteering for this mission and pushed myself throughout my entire time in combat.

Some men fought tooth and nail to never leave the security of Forward Operating Base (FOB) Speicher. They became known as FOBBITs. A

FOBBIT is a soldier who never leaves the security of the FOB. They are individuals who serve a year-long tour and never raise their weapon, and never hear machine gun fire. In the opinion of many, they do not perform their job as a soldier.

I fully understand that there are supply jobs, administrative jobs, maintenance jobs, and desk jobs that do not require kicking in doors and blowing up munitions, but during the first years of the Iraq war everyone was subject to combat. Combat is a soldier's number one job. Bottom line, we are first and foremost trained to fight bad guys. Some uniformed soldiers cowered at these ideas. These FOBBITs were real, and they were living among us.

> Jen, I had a cushy job later in my military career, but I was never, I mean never, a FOBBIT.

From Easter through Thanksgiving of 2004, I fell in on Trailblazer route clearance missions and led my team of five men from Ohio, alongside the established teams from North Dakota. We were joined by two other teams of six, also from Ohio. There were a total of eighteen of us that had volunteered for Trailblazer, and a fourth team was put together about 45 days later.

While most of the Construction Engineers from the 216th Engineer Battalion carried out their original missions of operating heavy equipment, digging in, building bridges and re-paving runways, a small number of Ohio soldiers helped clear nearly 200 IED's off the roads, alongside the N.D. Guardsmen. N.D. had written the doctrine on route clearance, but some Ohio boys were significantly changing the face of it with our engineer equipment.

And so, I became a part of Task Force Trailblazer and the route clearance mission during my Iraq deployment. I did it and I excelled at it, and was recognized for my actions with trinkets that are part of the ribbon rack on my dress uniform. However, what I would lose to the Trailblazer mission was worth more than any award I could ever receive.

IF IT WAS possible, I got used to the adrenaline that came with the insanity of the route clearance mission. Hearing the whiz of a bullet pass by became commonplace in 2004. Coffee was never needed. The probability of pissing my pants was higher if my bladder was even partially full. And I did. Many of us did.

I was driven by adrenaline… a hormone that was produced by my own body in an attempt to keep me alive. There was so much adrenaline produced by Trailblazer, it literally hurt to come down from it. In turn, I became extremely addicted to it.

Adrenaline is the name of a skeleton in my closet that still makes his appearance periodically. Sometimes, I have to take a triple look at Adrenaline just to see him clearly. But by allowing him to lead me, I am certain he saved my life a couple different times.

Jennifer, meet Adrenaline.

ADRENALINE ADAPTATION

Adrenaline naturally stimulates and raises testosterone and androgen hormones in young men. My body was producing an overabundance of natural steroids as a way to cope with the war. Adding the Trailblazer mission to the already maxed out lifestyle I was living in Iraq would push me physically and mentally to previously unattainable heights. One step further, one more nail pounded, one more push-up. Drive on soldier.

I was a ripped stud running five miles in sub forty minutes, and able to do ninety push-ups in under two minutes. Sometimes, I felt like if allowed I would have just kept on going forever. I was off the charts on my Army physical fitness test and was being judged on an extended scale, scoring over the normal maximum of 300. Having been a collegiate level swimmer I was used to being physically capable of nearly anything. But my experience in Iraq surpassed that fitness level by a landslide. It was completely amazing how physically able I was. I felt unbeatable, supernatural and raw, with Viking like power.

Supercharged by the constant flow of adrenaline through my veins, I felt unstoppable.

When it was time for me to actually relax after Trailblazer missions, I simply slept. I crashed so hard during my days off, it was unreal. I will never, ever sleep like that again. Death itself will bring less rest than the sleep that came after the combined stress of those missions. During one occasion, my roommates actually picked up my entire bed while I was in it and moved me. They proceeded to bang apart two metal bunk beds with metal hammers within ten feet of where I lay. They checked my pulse because they couldn't believe I never budged with the racket they were making. Sleeping from directly after lunch on Sunday until my Monday morning workout at 0430 was common during Trailblazer.

I also sang in the soldier's choir on Sunday mornings when I was on FOB Speicher. It helped to take my mind off the daily grind. It was an odd combination that makes me chuckle today. I blew up bombs, got shot at, and sang in the church choir. And sometimes all of those things took place within the same 24 hour period. I knew I had better be right with God, because every day might have been my last.

As a Battalion, the 216th Engineers experienced three of our own KIA. Samuel Bowen was KIA by an RPG explosion on July 7th 2004. You will never be forgotten. One of my longtime friends and fellow cross-level to the 216th Engineers from Norwalk was in a hummer that was completely destroyed by an IED on August 20th 2004. My friend miraculously survived the attack, but the explosion took Charles L. Wilkins III and Ryan A. Martin. Both were KIA. You will never be forgotten.

Purple Heart recipient Mike Romed was in a vehicle ten yards in front of mine when the IED that nearly killed him went off. Countless others were injured within a few yards of me in some form or another, many of them also garnering Purple Hearts.

While I was on Trailblazer missions, we were ambushed multiple times. During one particular ambush, a bullet or a piece of shrapnel that was destined for my head had cracked the glass, but for some reason did not penetrate. Many other bullets had penetrated glass just like it. In another incident a piece of IED shrapnel as large as the palm of my hand inexplicably stopped in a sand bag, inches from me.

IED shrapnel that was stopped by a sandbag.

These are only a few of the incidents. There were many others, and all of them were very, very real. Thankfully, I was never seriously physically injured. All of these incidents, however, took their eventual toll on me in other ways. In ways that were not seen by the naked eye.

Over time, I began to notice that my perception of things around me was changing. Basic principles and values that I grew up believing were being questioned inside my head. The day to day norm became high intensity destruction, and experiencing some death was inevitable. I, and all the "wonderful" thoughts inside my head, were being held together loosely by a constant adrenaline rush.

From a young age, I was taught that there is nothing more valuable than a human life. I still believe that today, although my ideas about life and death are now slightly jaded due to my experiences. Other humans trying to kill you, or taking the life of another, was not something for which I had planned. The knowledge of how to deal with that type of intensity on a daily basis happens mostly in fiction. It can be done, but it certainly brings changes to a man's mind along with it.

The first changes I began to notice were in reference to what I thought a human being was physically and mentally capable of. In my head, I could seemingly do it all. So, why couldn't everyone else? I began to actually believe I was somehow better than my fellows. The FOBBITs became cowards to me. The guys who were simply doing their jobs, and doing them well, as carpenters and equipment operators, etc., were mentally placed beneath me.

They were not putting themselves in harm's way day after day. When was it going to be their turn to give to this war like I was giving? I developed a dangerous and superior mindset full of suspicion toward others. And I disturbingly began to believe I was unstoppable.

It was a very dark and twisted way to think, and I seemingly had no control over it. I expected the absolute best out of everyone around me because I was dedicated to giving my very best. I believed whole heartedly in fighting the Al-Qaeda bad guys. Good vs. Evil. I was in the midst of the most important battle of my life. I was going to win this war and build the bridge across the cove to my childhood fortress, damn-it. Why wasn't everyone else capable and willing to do the same? With blinders on and a new bad attitude, I charged forward.

Specifically, this is how I came to the realization that I was changing. My Grandfather was one of the greatest men I have ever known. He taught my own Father everything he knew, who passed some of those gifts on to me. After Grandma had passed a few years earlier, Grandpa was having trouble with everyday life and its tasks. So, my parents moved in with him while I was overseas. My parents still live in my Grandparent's house today, where my Dad grew up, out on the farm When I go home today, I go to the farm, not to the house in Holiday Lakes that I knew as my home while growing up.

My Grandfather, Arthur Capell passed away while I was in Iraq.

When I heard the news of my Grandfather's passing, it didn't strike me as it should have. If I had pushed for it, I'm fairly certain I would have been able to go home for his funeral. I cannot explain the reasons why, but I didn't go home or push for the opportunity. I don't fully remember or understand all the details, but I didn't grieve at all. I didn't shed one tear. I never even told any of my fellow soldiers about my own Grandfather's passing until much later.

Not another word was spoken. Radio silence…

I didn't recognize my reception of this sad news as being odd until about sixty days later when my wife at the time, Fi, told me that my dog Kallie had grown a tumor. Kallie had a series of horrendous seizures while I was away from home and had to be put to sleep. I bawled for days and fell into a deep depression upon hearing the news of my puppy. But I still never grieved for the loss of my Grandfather. It was only after my dog died that I recognized I was going through some interesting and tough times inside my own head.

Jennifer, even though the context is certainly disturbing, the human mind is fascinating. Attempting to understand, and exploring how I got here is very interesting to me.

At the very same time that I raised the standard of what I thought a human was physically and mentally capable, I had lowered the value of a human life. Dealing with the death and destruction around me had caused me to diminish the importance I held for all human life, even those held most dear to me.

Did I care for my dog more than my Grandpa? Of course not! But my actions and emotional responses, or lack thereof, made it seem that way. It was as if I was a vampire and didn't have a reflection in the mirror anymore. How could I be emotionless during times when my emotions should have been extensive? The loss of emotion was both alarming and strange. It felt odd to feel nothing. Realizing I couldn't process normal emotions correctly was quite disturbing to me.

As you know, Jennifer, in September, 2017 while on my third deployment, my Grandfather on my Mother's side passed away. Within three hours of hearing of Papa's death, I had purchased a $1200 plane ticket home for his funeral. I would not make the same mistake twice with regards to family.

In Iraq, and especially on Trailblazer missions, there was no time for self-reflection or healing. I had IED's to uncover and a war to win. I was in this war to win it. Again with blinders on, I charged forward. In retrospect, it was at this moment that I should have taken a deeper look inside my psyche. Or better yet, I should have sought out a professional to help me do so. Hindsight is truly 20/20.

Adrenaline and the stressors of Task Force Trailblazer had created a disturbing mental psychosis inside of me.

Absence of expected emotional reactions facilitated the manifestation of one single emotion. ANGER! Because I didn't feel grief for the loss of my Grandfather, and because I didn't feel sadness concerning the horrors of the everyday struggle between the war and humanity, I was angry at myself. Having the perception that they were not trying as hard as I was, I was angry at my fellow soldiers. I was angry at my command for no apparent reason at all. I was simply angry.

I also began to develop a deep hatred and prejudice toward the Iraqi people, and certainly toward radical jihadist Muslims and Al-Qaeda. Not being able to differentiate between them, I conveniently placed them all into a single box inside my head. There was no time to figure that kind of thing out. Denying the mission complete concentration, or focusing on humanity for even a split second, could cause it to be your last.

The fact was that if these were normal circumstances or a single experience, I would have felt sadness, horror, and remorse for the situations I was confronted with. These were not normal circumstances, and they were happening all around me, on a daily basis. A rational person cannot live with those feelings continuously over a long period of time. So I created my own, anger laced superior mindset to cope with all those issues I could not deal with. I wouldn't attempt to fully understand the issues or my mindset, until many years later.

Keeping the passion for absolute physical prowess at the maximum level, exercise was seemingly my only release. I challenged my physical abilities like an Olympic athlete. A friend of mine and I once did 1000 push-ups in a single day just because we wanted a challenge.

Also, just to see if we could do it, we rode 200 miles on stationary bikes on one of our days off. It took us eleven miserable hours. Eleven hours on a stationary bike, focused on pedaling faster and further than the blast concussion of a 155mm artillery round. If I could go faster and if I was stronger, then the blast wouldn't get to me. This physical intensity added to the mental intensity that came with the mission. It was all absolutely ludicrous. Every... single... day.

What was going on outside of my head while on Trailblazer was of much the same intensity. While we drove slowly along the side of the road looking for their IED's, our enemy found adaptive and quite creative ways to attempt to end our lives. Putting explosives inside a camel carcass is just one sickening example of the extreme measures they took. They actually utilized the roadkill for jihad!

Trailblazer's tactics dictated that we push a layer of dirt with a bulldozer while trying to unearth a buried IED, or shooting a few rounds at a suspected IED in hopes that it would detonate out of our range. If it didn't detonate, one of us would actually walk up to it, confirm it was an IED, and place pre-primed explosive charges onto the IED. It was pure madness.

Before Trailblazer, the U.S. Army did not have a training program that included both demolitions teams and heavy equipment operation. It is now the standard operating procedure for training at the Army Explosives Ordinance Disposal (EOD) School. Nowadays, soldiers perform route clearance with blast protective Mine Resistant Ambush Protected (MRAP) vehicles. We had only hillbilly plate steel armor hanging off our doors, and sandbags piled up around us. It was something, but it wasn't much when stacked against the explosion caused by a couple 155mm artillery rounds daisy chained (several rounds tied together for a single, larger explosion) together by an adaptive enemy.

I hope I have been able to convey the recklessness we lived with on a daily basis, and the disturbance that the Trailblazer insanity advanced within my head. War is inherently not normal. The Trailblazer mission was a special kind of not normal. Today, no one would even think of asking a group of young men to do what we did in 2004. If ordered to do so, a soldier's reply would go something like this: "You want me to do what? Clear IED's with a bicycle? Are you insane?"

Yes, yes it was…

This next statement will probably come across as extremely bizarre. While Trailblazer was maximum insanity… it was also glorious. I loved all of it! Every single step of maximum intensity and every single instant my life was on the line was magnificent. I loved the power, the muscle, and the physical prowess. I loved the adrenaline, the danger, and the global cause we were fighting for. Pushing the envelope on my own life, one adrenaline riddled moment at a time, was fantastic.

Though it certainly has its Hollywood imperfections, reference the movie "The Hurt Locker". Like the lead character in the movie, I too, couldn't get enough of the madness. My country and my fellow soldiers depended on me do my very best. I had unknowingly placed the weight of the entire war on my shoulders. In my mind's eye, there was no other way to survive. I pressed myself daily for one more push-up, one more mile, and one more IED diffused. I loved every single crazy and angry moment with my skeleton Adrenaline. I was undeniably and certifiably an Adrenaline junky.

THE CULMINATING events which explain Task Force Trailblazer's madness and how it truly affected my persona, took place at Forward Operating Base (FOB) O'Ryan. The events at O'Ryan didn't coincide with a planned completion date for my stint on Trailblazer. According to my orders, I was supposed to continue with route clearance for the remainder of my deployment. Although Trailblazer continued on, the stories of explosions and bleak humanity that follow actually guaranteed the end of my participation on the mission.

These next few are some of the toughest letters that I have written to you, Jennifer.

FORWARD OPERATING BASE (FOB) O'RYAN, FOREWORD

Forward Operating Base O'Ryan was just off of Main Supply Route (MSR) Tampa, about fifty miles north of Bagdad. It was just south of FOB Anaconda and Balad, Iraq. MSR Tampa was the most heavily travelled interstate within Iraq. During my six week stint at O'Ryan, we successfully cleared forty or more IED's. We averaged almost one IED a day! Nearly every single day for six weeks straight, I was on a mission with intensity levels above the normal chaotic madness. Performing the mission was madness in itself, but finding an IED added to the intensity. Because if we found one, we had to deal with it.

While I was on O'Ryan, it was sometimes difficult to really understand who my "boss" was. I was with another unit and on a mission that was not organic to Construction Engineers. In addition, FOB O'Ryan was off the radar to my Ohio Command until they were told by North Dakota that I was headed there. Repeatedly, I was tossed around the Iraqi countryside on missions that didn't have any real command structure. There was no one checking up on me. And because I couldn't seem to properly cope with the emotions inside my head, that feeling of being alone became encased with hardened anger, just like all the others.

I had been searching for bombs since shortly after seeing the pink mist in my first firefight, on Easter Sunday 2004. It was now Halloween, and I was on FOB O'Ryan continuing my mission with Trailblazer. There were a few breaks in that seven month stretch for other engineering missions, but all of the white knuckle madness had inevitably taken its toll on me.

JENNIFER, meet KaBoom, aka Qunbala, the Arabic word for bomb. He is an exploding skeleton in my closet, with a single deadly purpose. Don't be alarmed when he explodes right in front of you. Since he is already dead, he can reassemble his bones and explode over and over again. We, on the other hand, only get one shot.

HOWE WE KABOOM

The amount of readily available munitions for Al-Qaeda to utilize as IED's in the area around FOB O'Ryan was preposterous. There were literally tons of large munitions simply lying around the countryside. As an American soldier who utilized countless control measures for all munitions back home, I found it absurd to discover 155mm artillery rounds just lying around. But they were everywhere. One of the jobs belonging to an engineer demolitions team was to gather these munitions and detonate them in a controlled blast. The more of them we got rid of, the less were available for deadly IED's.

Once, during off duty hours on FOB O'Ryan, a group of four men including myself were playing cards around a thin collapsible card table inside a canvas tent. A fifth guy, Fred, pulled out his blade and began to sharpen it. Every good soldier has a minimum of one knife on him at all times. Fred, however, had a knife for each day. Soon the conversation turned to passing each other's favorite blades around the table, and sharing stories about how that particular knife skinned the largest whitetail buck in its respective owner's township.

The cards were forgotten for the time being by everyone except an intimidating Lakota Indian from North Dakota with the last name of Howe. Yes, an American Indian named Howe. I'm sure he heard the joke a few times, but never after he stood up. Very few men would dare make the joke while he towered over them. He was an absolute giant of a man.

Howe was ignoring the knife exchange for the moment, although his own blade was in the rotation. He was focused on making a card pyramid on the shaky card table we circled. He didn't make it very far when a concussion blast ripped through the tent blowing all of the cards into the air. An explosive "ka-boom" came along with the concussion wave. I thought we were taking incoming mortars. The cards blowing over, the sound, and the faint whistle in the air from the concussion blast could have easily been mistaken for incoming mortars.

The repetitive sights and sounds of war become less and less effective in triggering the fear factor found in your psyche. I remember my first mortar attack early in March 2004 on FOB Speicher. I ran as fast as I could for shelter in one of the concrete and sandbag fortified pits after hearing the first explosion. Much later in the deployment, a few of us were on the roof of a building, smoking some very nice Cuban cigars and enjoying the calm of darkness. Suddenly, glowing tracer rounds flew closely over our heads like a fireworks display on the fourth of July. We watched them as five or more mortars landed just beyond their effective distance. Well into the war, we did not even think about seeking cover form the attack. They were really good cigars.

This explosion on O'Ryan, however, was not one that you'd risk keeping your cigar for. It was especially close. Actually feeling the concussion from a blast was fundamentally different than just hearing it. Four of us, knives in hand, and Howe wielding the ace of hearts, instinctively dove underneath the card table inside the canvas tent as if it would provide us some sort of blast protection. Fred stabbed me in my left arm with Tuesday, his knife for that day. One of the guys had an eight inch tear up his pant leg from one of our blades, but it never broke his skin. We were lucky none of us needed stitches, after diving into and fighting for the same four square feet of space.

As the playing cards floated to the ground and settled over all of us, Howe began to chuckle heartily. "Controlled blast, you assholes," he laughed.

Howe was right. We all looked at our watches from our heap of humanity. The controlled blast was scheduled to be detonated just about now.

Over the last several days, we had taken part in prepping various munitions for disposal in a controlled blast. As part of the preparation we dug a hole with a dozer that was fifteen feet wide by forty feet long and fifteen feet deep. We brought every munition that we had found in the area, and placed them into that hole. The blast site was in the middle of nowhere desert, about a mile from FOB O'Ryan. Soldiers on the midnight shift had been put in charge of the actual detonation.

The munitions had been primed with at least 50, maybe 75 1-lb. blocks of C4 explosives. Each 1-lb. brick had its own individual blasting cap. Some were buried among the various rounds and some were left on top. They were all then tied into a ring-main of detonating cord (det-cord), with a duel ignition system. Through this process we would be destroying nearly 1000 potential IED's.

The morning after the detonation, at first light, we drove out to the blast sight and discovered that the crater may have actually struck oil! The pit must have been 50 - 60 feet deep and a football field in diameter. We knew it was going to be a monster of an explosion, but holy shit!

My stories about knives are now limited to this single one. It's forevermore about that time when I was stabbed by Fred after a massive explosion, and how we "struck oil". This story certainly tops that of the biggest buck. It's a good one indeed. I'd guess that four other men share the same story as well.

PEANUT BUTTER

ONE OF the more horrific human stories of Forward Operating Base O'Ryan, or the entire war in general for me, was that of a young boy we called Peanut Butter.

Peanut Butter waved us down one morning while we were on a route clearance mission alongside route Tampa. He informed us of a munitions stockpile that we eventually seized and control detonated. These artillery rounds were part of what was blown up in the "KaBoom" story. The men on the engineer team gave Peanut Butter some candy and some peanut butter packets from a Meal Ready to Eat (MRE) as a simple gesture of kindness. The boy mistakenly understood our gifts to him as a controlled exchange process. In his eyes, if he gave us IED munitions, he would receive peanut butter in return.

Imagine a boy carrying a 60-lb live ordinance that was twenty inches long and five inches in diameter to within fifteen feet of a heavily travelled highway. Then he'd just sit there waiting for us to come rolling along. He'd spurt out of the bushes or from behind a rusty shack when he saw us moving laboriously alongside the road in our own search for deliberately placed munitions. After our original exchange, he would periodically show up alongside the road with two or three more artillery rounds that were as large as a man's thigh. He brought us bombs in exchange for some candy, a pack of crackers and some peanut butter.

The thought of this little boy and what he did gives an idea of the oppression that the Iraqi people were enduring. The years of Saddam Hussein's dictatorship, and now under Al-Qaeda, were simply awful. Tyranny ran rampant across the Arabian portion of the Iraqi countryside.

Although we tried not to become attached to Peanut Butter, and attempted in translation to tell the little boy not to bring any more 'qunbala' for fear of his and his family's lives, he continued to do so. We couldn't just leave the artillery rounds he brought to us laying there. For a month, he became part of our lives in the area we patrolled.

The qunbala for peanut butter exchange process continued. Until one day it didn't.

None of us truly know what happened to Peanut Butter. He disappeared after a firefight broke out in the village where he and his family resided. Our original gifts were intended to be innocent and simple acts of kindness, but more than likely contributed to the disappearance of Peanut Butter. Although he disappeared permanently from our roadside excursions, he will forever hold a spot inside my heart.

The absence of Peanut Butter from our missions added to my internal anger. Although I am certain he was on everyone's mind, not another word was spoken of him. Radio silence...

Howe and Peanut Butter

PUSHING MY MIND WITH A BULLDOZER

OPERATING A bulldozer was about the most fun endeavor a soldier could have in the world's largest sandbox. However, this was not the case when utilizing a bulldozer as a bomb sniffing dog. My hands were constantly sweaty and white knuckled on the steering levers controlling the tracks and blade defilade. The mission required the driver to inch along with the dozer blade about six inches underground, essentially scraping the surface of the ditch. The intent was to dig up buried qunbala before they were detonated upon an unsuspecting convoy.

The obvious issue with this process was that they could also be detonated by our enemies upon us, or somehow triggered by the dozer and detonated. And sometimes they were. I actually peed myself a little a couple different times, after the concussion of an IED rocked my frame. No one would ever know, because we ended up soaked from sweat inside the 100 degree cabs of the vehicles we were in. I have forgotten how many times I witnessed an IED detonate. The single most profound incident that still rings in my head, is contained in the following story.

One morning while operating the dozer alongside MSR Tampa outside FOB O'Ryan, an IED went off about fifty yards in front of me. It completely engulfed a civilian Toyota pick-up truck and lifted it fifteen feet into the air in a blast of concussive flames. It also knocked over a tractor trailer and started it on fire. Like our training dictated, we halted and prepared ourselves for possible secondary attacks which may have been directed at us.

A few minutes later, after the threat was deemed over, I dismounted the dozer with my loaded M16 rifle in hand. Immediately after turning the corner around the edge of the five foot tall dozer blade and crouching down beneath its peak for cover, I noticed qunbala. Right there in the dirt and sand, directly beneath my knees glaring upwards, was a 155mm artillery round with a wire protruding from underneath it. My brain recognized my predicament immediately and correctly. I was sitting on a bomb.

I had done everything correctly. I had followed all the procedures that had been taught to me. I had fought valiantly and had not made any grave mistakes. I was physically and mentally prepared. I was fully trained in demolitions and various other essential combat skills. I had given my all toward the success of our mission and the overall goal of winning this war. I was a living recruiting poster for the Army.

Despite all of that, the instant I recognized the artillery round at my feet, I collapsed next to it on the hardened sandy earth in a sweating heap of horror. The 155mm round lay twelve inches from my trembling knees, in the waves of rolling sand and dirt that were in front of my bulldozer's blade.

I just knelt there in complete desolation and shock. I'm not certain whether I cried, laughed, shuddered, screamed, or all of them at once. I may have hugged qunbala, I really have no idea. I was completely overwhelmed as every plausible emotion pulsed through my head, to the rhythm of my palpating heart. My heart was thumping loudly between my ears. It was the only sound I heard. I was unsure if I was going to live another second. Both my mind and body had run out of Trailblazer intensity. The mission seized me. I was broken. My mind retreated from my present surroundings and I was no longer in Iraq, no longer fighting, no longer running, no longer hiding, and no longer conscious of my current predicament.

Was the IED still rigged to the detonator? "Thump, thump," pounded my heart. Had I been pushing it for the last mile? Thump, thump. Had it just made its way out of the ground? Thump, thump. Was it a secondary device meant to detonate on us when we halted? Thump, thump. Was the first blast just a decoy IED? Thump, thump. Was I going to die? Thump… thump…

Overwhelmed with every question and every demand being made on me, I fully succumbed to the constant pressure and the flow of adrenaline. My knees literally buckled under the 80-lbs. of ammunition, bullet proof vest, and other protective gear I carried. The neurons inside my brain quit firing. There were no mental or physical connections being made. I had lost my ability to think. I had no ability to reason. Leaning back against the blade of the dozer and my rifle, I rocked helplessly back and forth. Defenseless and useless against qunbala, I shattered into incapable pieces. Entirely alone. At that moment the war had taken me into its depths. I stared blankly at the smoke rolling upward from the truck that had exploded a few minutes prior. I was not even cognizant of my own physical location.

Thump, thump, pounded my heart. I was lost. Thump, thump. We had detonated… thump, thump …nearly 1000 munitions days earlier. Thump, thump. How could there possibly be more? Thump, thump. This will never… thump, thump …ever… thump, thump …ever end… thump… thump…

After what seemed like an eternity, my mind arose from its blank stupor. But I was still physically frozen, kneeling and leaning against the dozer blade. As I recovered, I broke free from my paralysis and slowly placed the muzzle of my rifle against the blade of the dozer. I took a single, deep, controlled and steady breath. And one more time, I focused just enough to face the unnerving qunbala. As I cowered above it, droplets of sweat, possibly mixed with tears, ran down my nose and dripped on the artillery shell's metal casing. My trembling hands dug around the piece of artillery, not knowing if my mere touch would set it off. It was as large as my thigh. In a fit of final desperation and rage, I forcefully yanked the wire from underneath the munition and collapsed against the dozer blade once again.

An unknown amount of time had passed when I was aroused by the sound of a familiar voice. "Water, here drink some water."

Howe handed me one of the plastic water bottles from inside the cab of the dozer. I dropped it into the sand. In an attempt to pick it up, I fumbled again. Howe gave me the bottle again, and on my third attempt at a drink, my hands couldn't grip the cap effectively enough to open it.

"How long have you been sitting next to this little guy?" he asked, referring to qunbala while he opened the water bottle for me.

"I… I. I don't. Man… I don't …I don't even know man?"

Not another word was spoken. Radio silence…

The one that didn't go off was the one that finally got me.

On our way back to FOB O'Ryan I rode shotgun in a canvas topped hummer, snapped a few photos, and whispered silently to myself, over and over. "Please God! I beg of you to deliver me from this place."

That was my last Task Force Trailblazer mission. I would never search for another qunbula. As a man who puts my entire being into the things I want to accomplish, Trailblazer had sucked every ounce of effort from me. I was as dry as the Iraqi desert which was trying to kill me. I needed a couch, a regular dosage of Advil and some healthy servings of homemade chicken noodle soup.

Constantly pushing the limits, I had finally found my own breaking point.

Trailblazer. FOB O'Ryan and the dozer that pushed my limits.

Tractor trailer still on fire well after the IED had gone off.

I WAS NEVER the same after my final duel with qunbala. "The one that didn't go off" was the one that literally pushed me over the edge. I simply couldn't take any more of the intensity and insanity. I had broken. However, I was still arrogant, and proud to have outlasted many others who had removed themselves prior to my long overdue exit. One step further. Suck it up buttercup. Drive on Soldier.

VIGILANT GUARDIAN

On a recommendation from Howe, who discussed "the one that didn't go off" with me, and then with his North Dakota command, I went back to FOB Speicher and "took a break" from Trailblazer. Howe's discussion ended with his command. So, because I was detached from the 216th and assigned to the N.D. Guard for Trailblazer, word of my incident with "the one that didn't go off" never made it back to my unit.

In addition, the timing for me to return to Speicher was right. Every soldier had the opportunity to take two weeks of leave (vacation). Months ago I had scheduled my stint home over the Thanksgiving holiday, and my birthday. I was never asked the question why I returned "early", because I was scheduled to go home on leave. So as far as my unit leadership was concerned, I had simply finished the Trailblazer mission.

Mere thoughts of qunbala continued to make my heart beat faster. Thump, thump. But the warrior in me said, "Why did anyone ever have to know that I broke down under pressure?" Thump, thump. I didn't really care to have the perceived stigma of weakness branded permanently on my helmet. Thump, thump. Everything seemed to fall into place naturally. Thump, thump. Not another word was spoken about "the one that didn't go off". Thump... thump... Radio silence...

On my return to Speicher I helped Harry Nobel with the project he was working on at the time. The 216th Construction Engineers were building some forty foot span trusses for a Tactical Operations Center. It was a great relief to swing a hammer and see the fruits of my labor. I was able to get back into a regular sleep schedule, and was soon out running a few miles every morning at 0430. I was back at it, and never really slowed down since Easter Sunday. Even that damn IED, "the one that didn't go off", seemingly couldn't stop me.

Screw you, qunbala.
                                    - Joel A. Capell

After building those trusses with Harry Nobel, I dug in some Marines on the three day trip to Fallujah that I wrote about previously. Then I went home.

The short break from the war was magnificent. I napped on the couch, after having my fill of homemade chicken noodle soup. I do remember having some trouble sleeping, but passed that off as readjusting to the eight hour time difference between the Iraqi and Eastern Standard time zones. I didn't talk to anyone about the war or the incidents that haunted me while I was home. A chivalrous man couldn't burden his family with those worrisome details. So I didn't. The time was not right to unload the weight from my shoulders. Knowing I had to go back, I maintained my radio silence and kept the intense memories to myself.

Two weeks (ten days home due to travel time) wasn't enough time to catch up on the sleep I was in dire need of, and before I knew it, I was headed back into the fight. But it was enough recovery time to get my game face back on. Qunbala and the war had taken a lot from me, but had not taken all of me. Drive on soldier.

Returning to Iraq in early December after the short visit home was simply awful. Saying good bye again, and this time having a picture in my head of what I was returning to, made leaving again even worse than the first time.

Jen, here are a few words paraphrased by myself from a respected man I met overseas.

When people talk to me about a deployment, they always mention that it must be very difficult to be separated from my family for so long. I concur, it certainly is. But then I make sure to explain to them that the hardest part of a deployment is not actually being separated. Because once I am "gone", I have another family that I am surrounded by while I'm overseas in my military family. Leaving my real family behind, knowing that they will not have the same support group that I do, is the hardest part... the hardest part is leaving.

- Anonymous

In addition to the obvious returning to war gloom I was experiencing, an entire wave of new coalition replacement forces were entering Iraq. They crowded the roads with inexperience just prior to the December holidays. A couple of the new units had soldiers who were hurt pretty badly while convoying their way north out of Kuwait. One of the units took a wrong turn and was catastrophically ambushed in an Iraqi town they should have never even been in. The American death toll was high in late 2004.

Operation Vigilant Guardian was the 1st Infantry Division's answer to the incoming transportation problems. It was a convoy security mission that was to be put together with a few seasoned guys from each unit in the area. The mission would be to escort convoys from Kuwait to required destinations in Iraq.

Once again, having no squad as an E-6, I was chosen as one of the representatives for this new mission from the 216th Engineer Battalion. Twenty soldiers in total from various units, three from the 216th, including myself, were given ten brand new armored hummers with less than twenty miles on the odometer. The plastic was still on the seats. We were also given five new MK-19 automatic grenade launchers, five new M2 50cal machine guns, and enough ammunition to level a city block as part of the package deal.

Secretary of Defense Rumsfeld's promise of better equipment had been delivered. These armored hummers were the first we had ever seen. They were true war machines. Actually being able to mount the new weapons into built in protective turrets was impressive. The vehicles certainly gave us a newfound piece of mind. It would be nice to sit somewhat protected behind a couple inches of bulletproof glass and over an inch of hardened steel.

But why me? Why was I the one headed back into danger again? It made me angry that with only seven weeks left in Iraq, I would be performing another dangerous mission with a group of protection "gun trucks", escorting convoys. I had spent seven months on Trailblazer, been blown up, pissed my pants, lost my mind to "the one that didn't go off", and had seen the pink mist. Take one of these FOBBIT's who have never even left the confines of the base! I didn't want to do this anymore! I was immediately angry again.

A good friend of mine, JR, had been performing a very similar "gun truck" mission escorting transportation convoys the entire time he had been in country. He knew the ropes of this new assignment better than anyone. However, the convoys we would be escorting would not be normal everyday convoys. Every single mission, we would be escorting new soldiers into Iraq, and that would come with natural drawbacks.

I was told that I was chosen because I knew the ways of the road better than anyone. I had travelled them repeatedly and had the right experience for the new mission. This was all true. The same was true with JR. We did know the roads better than anyone else. But not only was I to be part of the mission, this time I was chosen to lead these twenty men on this mission. It was an honor and a huge responsibility. The lives of twenty Vigilant Guardians and the lives of the new units we would escort would soon depend on me as their convoy security leader.

Vigilant Guardian was a hodge-podge of experienced veterans who truly knew what they were doing. These guys had real wartime experience. There were no FOBBITs and I ran things accordingly. In addition to the experience we had on the mission, we also had these new Viking power armored hummers. This mission fit perfectly into my "I'm indestructible" head game.

The first two escort missions were flawless. The raw power that these new armored High Mobility Multipurpose Wheeled Vehicles or

HMMWV's (hummers) and turret mounted weapons brought to the table was evidently very intimidating to our enemy. I could feel the military supremacy run through my blood. To have authority over these men and the firepower that they had at their fingertips was awesome. And it was mindboggling. The muscle that Vigilant Guardian displayed was tremendous, but it reinforced my already dangerous mindset of superiority.

Although I was now the leader of ten Operation Vigilant Guardian gun trucks, I was not actually in charge of any of the convoys. The Commanding Officer of the units we escorted would have the reins of command throughout the time we travelled together. Vigilant Guardian was designed only to provide security, and direction if needed. When an incident occurred, it was the unit Convoy Commander's responsibility to report it, not mine. I didn't have to worry about all those mundane things that came with leading most military missions. I never had any paperwork to file and never had any groundwork to complete. All we needed was fuel and ammo. These were both charged to the account of the unit we were escorting.

Jennifer, nobody really cared much about paperwork during the early years of the war. It was about life or death back then.

Once again, I found myself on a mission where it was difficult for me to determine who my boss was at any given moment. This time, however, I figured out who my boss was very quickly. I had just turned 26 years of age over the Thanksgiving holiday, and I would be the boss! I had already seen the worst of the war and had pulled through it. Now, I didn't need to answer to anyone. There wasn't anyone there to listen or answer to anyway. Even though I was surrounded by military brothers, and had the confidence of a warrior, I felt alone. Again.

Our third trip from Kuwait into Iraq was about a week prior to Christmas. Fifteen minutes into the mission we had to come to a complete halt just across the border, because one of the new unit's gunners had failed to properly configure his 50cal weapon while putting it together. The four foot barrel of his M2 50cal had actually fallen off the body of the weapon and was spinning in the middle of the road. My confidence in this new unit was not very high.

I was rightfully pissed off! I gave the gunner more than just a piece of my mind. JR thankfully pulled me back from possibly striking a young Lieutenant, the gunner's Commanding Officer, after he ordered me to "back off", of his gunner.

My racing heart began to pound against the armored plates in my vest. Thump, thump. How in the hell does something like this happen? Thump, thump. Was this some kind of a joke to them? Thump, thump. Soldiers die because of mistakes like that! Thump, thump. If that gunner had fired his weapon with a loose barrel… thump, thump …it would have exploded in his face! Thump… thump…

Violent outbursts were not part of my normal character, but they were a part of my current character. I was wound so tight, I'm pretty sure I would have hit that Lieutenant square in the mouth if JR hadn't restrained me. That single moment of rage could have ended my military career.

Unstoppable and indestructible, I believed that I was somehow invulnerable to the hell surrounding me. And during the seven weeks of Vigilant Guardian, I let everyone I came into contact with know it.

After recouping the lost 50cal barrel, we continued our mission into Al-Qaeda country. Just north of Cedar II logistics hub on MSR Tampa, we slowed down to make a turn. Our convoy commander Lieutenant had been ordered by Transportation Command to take a specific route around Bagdad. TransCom controlled the route of every registered convoy on the road. All convoys coming out of Kuwait needed authorization from TransCom in order to get across the Kuwaiti border. There were several possible routes around the largest city in Iraq, but the one we were about to take was the worst. There were too many choke points and areas for possible ambush.

We made our turn to avoid downtown Bagdad, and headed safely northwest in a semicircle for the next 15-20 miles. Two miles prior to merging back onto route Tampa, we were forced to slow down while entering a populated area. This area was one of the identified choke points where we would be ripe for picking in an ambush.

Suddenly over the radio everyone heard someone scream, "Contact left, contact left! Should we return fire?"

"This is Victor-Gulf Six! Return fire!" I demanded over the communication waves. Victor-Gulf Six or V-G-6 was phonetic alphabet for Vigilant Guardian 6.

With those words, I commanded all of Vigilant Guardian and ten turret mounted weapons to reign havoc over anything and everything in our general nine o'clock direction. Ten months in this God forsaken country, and its constant attempt to kill me, were vindicated and avenged when those violent words passed my lips.

In the next 45 seconds, thousands of 50cal bullets and hundreds of MK-19 grenades created a concentrated barrage of firepower. We completely destroyed the building to our nine o'clock position. Fuck you, and the horse you rode in on. Fuck this place, fuck Al-Qaeda. Fuck you and you, and fuck you, too. The rage I had within me ran rampant through my blood and into my voice, commanding all to return fire. That rage transferred directly into the ringing in my ears from the U.S. military weapons letting loose above my head. The convoy came to a halt because its Vigilant Guardian gun trucks slowed down in order to flood hell upon our enemy.

The rules of engagement during my entire time in Iraq encouraged able soldiers to seek and destroy a verified threat. The introduction of the new armored HMMWV's mixed with my current mindset and the rules of engagement at the time, were all a recipe for what those who have never been there call a "misuse of power". In this instance, that label may have fit. I almost wanted a firefight. After all, what good was all the awesome firepower if we didn't get to use it? We did use it. I commanded the use of it. All of it. We found out very quickly that the capabilities of these war machines and the weapons were above our wildest expectations. Whatever threat there was from that general direction a minute ago didn't have a snowball's chance in hell.

"Cease fire! Cease fire! Q-R-F we're up. Follow my lead," I bellowed loudly over the radio.

Our designated Quick Reactionary Force (QRF) of three vehicles, including the one in which I was riding shotgun (front seat passenger), broke off from the convoy just as we had rehearsed many times. The QRF team was specifically designed to be a smaller more agile attack force, and to ensure the imminent threat to our convoy was neutralized.

My vehicle's driver drove right up the center, directly at the perceived threat. Two more Vigilant Guardian armored gun trucks followed. The first gun truck behind mine went left, and the second went to the right. We formed a 180 degree perimeter around the severely damaged building. We waited a minute, letting the smoke clear and dust settle, before dismounting to search the premises. I left the 50cal gunner in my vehicle for over watch. The driver remained as well, in case the need arose for a quick extract during our dismounted search.

The other two QRF vehicle drivers and passengers dismounted along with me. The five of us slowly approached the building. All three vehicle gunners in their protective turrets trained their eyes on the building toward which we were headed. Their fingers were at the ready position on the trigger.

No matter the circumstances, the intensity always stepped up when dismounting a protective vehicle. My heart felt like it was going to explode. It thumped wildly as I stepped out of my armored hummer.

Inside the building we found several casualties. The chances were very slim that anyone could have survived that bombardment. Just inside a window facing the road, a man whose frame was larger than the typical Iraqi was on the floor in a pool of blood. A shadow was cast over his head and shoulders. I could see him clearly only from his chest down. The blinding light coming through the window intensified the sight of unsettled dust particles floating in the otherwise dim building. The contrast in light and haze made it very difficult to see as we approached his lifeless body.

I moved slowly into the shadow line, finger on the trigger of my locked and loaded M16. In the instant my eyes adjusted to the darkness, I discerned that he was missing half of his face. The sight of his missing face startled me, but also sent a wave of relief over me, as it confirmed his death. We also came across a younger man and a few AK-47's. But we never saw any larger weapons.

Another figure among the deceased was a woman in full black burka dress. She was covered in black fabric from head to toe, with only a slit for her eyes. Which were still open and peering eerily, lifelessly into to the dim and dusty light. A small part of me wanted them to blink at me, but they did not. I was tired of the killing, the dead, the weapons, the bombs, and the burka. Normally, the eyes were the only sign of life that could be seen behind the full cover of a black burka. Her unblinking, dead, unresponsive eyes are another image that will stay with me until the day I die.

There may have been more casualties inside the building, but there were areas we could not enter because of the destruction we had caused. Maybe there were others? Maybe there were people who had somehow survived? We didn't stick around to find out. There was an entire convoy with 120 soldiers sitting on MSR Tampa, stagnantly waiting on us at this very moment. It was my job to deliver them safely to their destination. Duty calls... drive on soldier.

The dismounted QRF patrol and I returned to our vehicles. On the way back, JR and I shook hands in a gesture signaling that we were both alright. Upon entering my vehicle, I immediately radioed the young Lieutenant and told him that we would be returning to the convoy and to prepare to move out. That's exactly what we did.

The next thirty minutes were filled with radio chatter from everyone who had fired a weapon. They were reporting to the Lieutenant (LT) how much ammunition they had used. In turn, he would compile the total amount of ammunition needed for replacement at our next scheduled stopping point. A few of my Operation Vigilant Guardian gunners were completely out of ammo. They had let loose a year's worth of pent up frustration on that helpless building. Fuck you, and fuck you too. If I had been in a gunner's turret, I have no doubt I would have let my frustrations loose in the form of that bombardment as well.

While the requests for ammunition poured over the radio waves, all I could think about was the woman in the black burka. I had crossed paths with the black cat, and her piercing eyes will forever remain open in my mind.

We escorted the LT and his convoy up to FOB Danger in Tikrit, Iraq, where we met his advance party team. Like Pawpaw and I had done, the LT's team had come into Iraq a week prior to the rest of their unit. The team had living quarters already arranged for all 120 of the new men in the convoy.

As some of the men began to unload their gear, the LT pulled me aside and proceeded to read me the riot act for making his convoy stop in the middle of an ambush zone. As he yelled, my heart began to beat in between my ears. Thump, thump, was the only thing I actually heard, as the LT droned on. Thump, thump. Who in the hell does he think he is? Thump, thump. Doesn't he know who I am? Thump, thump. I have been through nearly eleven months of hell! Thump, thump. The nerve of this guy on his first day in country! Thump, thump. I was three seconds from breaking his nose four hours ago? Thump, thump. I would do it if he doesn't shut up! Thump… thump…

I let him drone on a little bit more about transportation safety and other stupid regulations. While he recited all the book answers for things he had no actual experience with, I heard only my heartbeat. Amazingly I held back the expletives, and my fists.

In between heartbeats, I noticed the air smelled of automotive grease, gasoline, and landfill. And whiffs of roadkill every fifth breath.

At the exact moment I had received enough ridicule from him, with a gesture for him to shut up, I yelled back at him very loudly from my smirking jaw, "Welcome to Iraq, Lieutenant!"

A moment later, the LT let go of his animosity and offered his hand. I extended my own arm and he shook my dirty fingered, stained and calloused hand. I accepted his peace offering and took particular notice of his well-rested eyes. It was uncommon to see eyes that were not yet sunken in and surrounded by dark circles. As we exchanged our single pleasantry from the trip, he relaxed his tone and thanked me for escorting him and his men safely.

I will remember his name forever. I saw it for the first time on his chest when he removed his body armor. Until this moment his name was just Lieutenant to me. His uniform name tape read "SMITH" in black, bold letters. How ironic I thought. The first guy that I met in Iraq after getting off the plane with Pawpaw was named Smith. And now, a year later, one of the last guys I would welcome to Iraq was also named Smith. The camouflage cover on his Kevlar helmet was brand new. All of his gear was spotless. When he took his armored vest off, he wouldn't even put it on the dusty ground. I didn't even bother taking my vest off anymore. I had actually worn it directly into the shower a few times over the past year.

I had become the war-torn soldier who I had met a year ago after getting off of the C-130 aircraft with Pawpaw. I was now the one with stained fingers, dirty smelly gear, was unshaven, had deeply sunken eyes full of anger, and lacked restful sleep. I was now the veteran introducing the new soldier to the war in Iraq.

The year had been rough on me. I had triumphed and fallen, and triumphed again and fallen deeper. I had won many battles with qunbala, and had lost at least one. I had given my very best in the form of constant dedication to mission. I had let lives continue by clearing IED's. I had also taken multiple lives.

"What in the hell is that smell?" Lieutenant Smith asked me.

"You'll get used to it. The entire country smells like this," was my intolerant answer.

Conversation was at a minimum. I was now the one who had lost personal skills over the last year of my life. I didn't want to talk to him. I knew that after the next twenty minutes, I would never see him again.

"Piss-off, Lieutenant", was what I wanted to say out loud, but the words remained within my head.

Not another word was spoken. Radio silence…

In the blink of an eye, LT Smith was gone and so was I.

Sometime during the second week of January, the 216th Combat Engineers and I passed my buddies in the Norwalk Guard unit. They were coming north into Iraq on Main Supply Route (MSR) Tampa, while we were on our way south, permanently. The sun would set its final day for me in that God forsaken place. I needed to go home.

Standing next to a hummer with a 50cal silhouetted gunner. Traffic was stopped behind us, due to spotting an IED on the road.

The following excerpts are from "Iraq: Politics and Governance", March 2016. They lay out a brief synopsis of events since 2005, when I left Iraq.

A series of elections began in 2005, (the elections were) after a one-year occupation period and a subsequent seven-month interim period of Iraqi self-governance that gave each community a share of power and prestige to promote cooperation and unity. A 55-member drafting committee, in which Sunnis were underrepresented, produced a draft constitution, which was adopted in a public referendum of October 15, 2005.

The 2005 elections did not resolve the Sunnis' grievances over their diminished positions in the power structure, and subsequent events reinforced their political weakness and sense of resentment. The bombing of a major Shiite shrine (Al Askari Mosque) in the Sunni-dominated city of Samarra (Salahuddin Province) in February 2006 set off major Sunni-Shiite violence that became so serious that many experts, by the end of 2006, were considering the U.S. mission as failing.

In early 2007, the United States began a "surge" of about 30,000 additional U.S. forces—bringing U.S. troop levels to a high of about 170,000. Citing the achievement of many of the agreed benchmarks and a dramatic drop in sectarian violence, the Bush Administration asserted that political reconciliation was advancing but that the extent and durability of the reconciliation would depend on further compromises among ethnic groups.

By the formal end of the U.S. combat mission on August 31, 2010, the size of the U.S. force was 47,000 and it declined steadily thereafter until the last U.S. troop contingent crossed into Kuwait on December 18, 2011.

Still, disputes over the relative claims of each community on power and economic resources permeated almost every issue in Iraq and were never fully resolved. These unresolved differences—muted during the last years of the U.S. military presence—reemerged in mid-2012 and have since returned Iraq to major conflict. (Katzman and Humud, 2016)

Thump, thump. This will never… thump, thump …ever… thump, thump …ever end… thump… thump…

VI

Pain & Whiskey

RETURNING HOME from war is possibly more difficult than war itself.

HOME FROM A PLACE NOT A STATE OF MIND

After a welcome back to the United States from the Hug Lady I was home in Ohio on Valentine's Day 2005. Finally home! Fi (my wife at the time) and I were on a second honeymoon and had a new commitment to each other found in my absence. Our marriage was rejuvenated naturally by my return. Early on, the man I had become was not clearly visible due to all the ribbons and flags and beers and celebrations.

About a month after my return Fi saw in me what I could not. Troubled, she told me repeatedly that I was a different man. No doubt she was just as confused as I was. We were told by many experts that I may in fact be a little different on my return. We both thought that it would pass, so we weren't too alarmed.

I was indeed different. The war had changed me, and the statements from my wife regarding these differences were certainly factual. But the way I dealt with my issues was definitely not a family oriented solution.

My family and co workers were not soldiers in my platoon. Everything was not life or death. But I evidently acted like it was. Full of anger and recklessness, still wound tight and extremely demanding, just like in Iraq I expected too much from everyone around me.

We thought I was possibly dealing with Post Traumatic Stress Disorder (PTSD). Because Fi asked me too, I sought council from a support group at a Veterans Affairs (VA), Community Based Outpatient Clinic (CBOC), and medical center. I hated those "therapy" sessions, and had trouble relating to any of the guys there. Truthfully, I had trouble relating to anyone. I was still fighting the war in my head and still had the adrenaline surges and energy required for Trailblazer. The guys at these sessions had all seemed to give up on everything, including themselves. They were all slumped over in their chairs and barely spoke a word. A complete opposite to them, I couldn't sit still and wouldn't shut up. But it seemed like my words were never heard. I didn't fit into the mold at the VA. I was diagnosed with nothing after several of these short sessions, and went on about my life.

During my first year home I didn't have many overly stressful nightmares, although I did have some moments of discomfort thinking about Iraq. I frequently dreamt about going back to my mission, where things were less confusing. The Army provided the basic life necessities, and Al-Qaeda understood me and I understood them. There were no bills, no emotions, and no normal everyday life stressors in combat.

In a peculiar way the Army is a very simplified life. And my perception of combat was the ultimate in black and white. Prior to the U.S. turning Iraq into a police state we were simply combatants. Soldiers who neutralized! And early in the war the Rules of Engagement still allowed us to do that very thing. The war in Iraq was not easy on me by any means, but it certainly streamlined my life into basic principles of survival. I actually missed it.

In an effort to occupy my mind and utilize the endless amounts of energy I had, I competed in my first sprint triathlon. I got third place overall. In my very first swim, bike, run race I got third place out of nearly 200 competitors! That gives an idea of my physical conditioning at the time.

According to my new home building contractor boss, I was the world's greatest employee. Requiring the best from my co-workers, I challenged them to perform to a higher standard and prided myself in outperforming everyone around me. I always carried one more 2x4.

I was an absolute asshole in many aspects. But my boss didn't care because I accomplished the tasks that no-one else wanted to do and asked for more of them at the end of the day. And each morning I reported back for duty fifteen minutes early. The Army reinforces and rewards both consistency and reliability. Those two characteristics go a long way in the world we live in. I was rewarded monetarily by my new boss for my drive and dedication. I was obviously outworking my co-workers and doing things they didn't want to do, but was no doubt resented because I received raises in pay rather quickly in comparison to most of them.

If "driven" was my middle name, "one step further" should have been my last name. Thank you, Sir, may I please have another? Another cookie or another lashing, I would take either in stride and always ask for more. Another beating, another dirty job, another party, another triathlon, another beer, I never took a break.

Just about the exact time Fi was attempting to tell me that I was a different man, she also informed me that she was pregnant. Isaac Arthur Capell was born nine months after my return home. His middle name was given in honor of the Grandfather who had passed away while I was in Iraq.

Isaac's bright shining smile distracted me from what I truly needed. Don't get me wrong, my firstborn son is one of the greatest miracles in my life. I love him more than I can express through words on paper. But the timing of Isaac's birth was centered directly in the middle of my struggles. Isaac made me happy, and that happiness momentarily delayed the inevitable downward spiral that was my life.

> Jennifer, this is a crass reality, both then and in retrospect. But I don't believe there is any other way to write about it. These are not easily discussed subjects, or times in my life. The truth is still the truth, no matter how painful.

Even after the birth of my son I still chose to follow a path that brought me closer to my rock bottom. The process was not pretty, and it unfortunately involved more lives than my own. I may never be able to completely forgive myself for the way I treated my family.

I'd occasionally pick up a six pack of beer for the evening and the first top was twisted off on the way home from the jobsite. That six pack quickly evolved into a six pack of tall-boys (16 oz.), with 2-3 downed before arriving home. At the recommendation of Fi, for more stability and less road time, I applied and was hired at the local lumber yard in my home town.

As the assistant store manager, I was asked by the district manager to clean the place up. During my tenure at the lumber yard there never was a store manager who was actually worth a damn. Three store managers in title only, were hired and fired. I was once again in a situation where I didn't have a boss. Essentially, I ran the store while discovering that I was a disgruntled and slightly dysfunctional new veteran. Dealing with customers all day didn't go so well for me. I'll just say I had a few issues with customer service. When a customer was upset about something and asked to see the manager, they got a piece of me. If a customer was a rude and loud asshole, I was twice the loud asshole they ever thought of being. The employees of the lumber yard were my new squad members. Don't disrespect my squad.

As an all American hero who had just spent a year detonating bombs, no task was impossible. Accomplishing exactly what was asked of me by the district manager, I cleaned the place up. Evidently, getting rid of old cull lumber and unclaimed windows and doors for a fraction of their original costs wasn't such a great idea economically. With my blinders on I failed to see how that was my problem. I wasn't asked to make money! Cleaning the place up was my task, so that is exactly what I did! The old inventory that I decided to get rid of had been sitting at that store for years, just rotting. They were lucky to have gotten any return on it at all. Our district manager still got his bonus that year, so it must have only slightly killed his profit margin. The storefront presentation truly shined after my time there. It shined like newly polished boots on a parade field.

I accomplished everything that was asked of me in my professional life. But where I continuously failed was in how to deal with people, and how to deal with myself. I was having a real tough time building respectable relationships due to my lack of emotion. The inability to form intimate bonds with others in my life was very tough on me after returning home. I have always been a very social person and enjoyed having close family and friends around whenever possible. It certainly was not easy on my marriage either.

During those first couple years home, I told many lumber yard customers whom I'd never met before where I thought they should go. Considering my actions toward people I didn't know, my family didn't stand a chance. While I was able to hold it together for the most part professionally and publically, where I truly suffered was at home. I needed excitement and craved change. Stability… I was not. If I was Dr. Jekyll at work, my family was getting all of my Mr. Hyde.

In addition to the lack of emotions, my skeleton Adrenaline was alive and well. He'd come bursting out in me every now and then. And my current answer to the high energy levels was riding my new Trek road bicycle twelve miles each way to work, every day possible. Exercise creates adrenaline-like endorphins, and any attempt to use some of that energy really just made me want more.

"The Walk", M16 and a 1-lb. block of pre-primed C4 explosive.
Current Mission: detonate the IED next to the tree.
Wearing the green Kevlar bomb "Gumby Suit".

There was literally an entire Army of veterans coming home from battle with symptoms not seen since the war in Vietnam. Symptoms that came from repeatedly having to do thing like make "The Walk", in the previous photo. Inexperienced doctors had never seen the raw symptoms indicating the post war issues we were having. They had just read about them in books, if even that. Adding to the inexperience, the policy of the VA at the time was one year of complete comprehensive care after returning from a combat zone. One year? One year barely got a soldier past the welcome home parties.

Multiple Good Idea Fairies had released their compounded wrath on the first waves of warfighters in the Global War on Terror. Personally, with no formally diagnosed issues, I could not receive any outpatient services after one year from the date of my return. As a combat veteran, I was unable to be treated by the VA. Many of us fit into this category. We never had much of a chance.

The VA has since changed their policy to five years comprehensive care after return. Since 2005, PTSD research and treatment plans have also changed drastically. We really were guinea pigs of the healthcare world.

We Engineers had performed the route clearance mission for 7-8 months, used hand placed explosives, and utilized unarmored equipment. Like the VA, the Army has also changed their policy. They have lowered the maximum time a soldier can continuously perform the route clearance mission during combat operations to six months. Today, the military has specialized EOD teams, with explosive placing robots, and highly protective MRAP vehicles. We were the guinea pigs of the military world as well.

Personally, other than noticing my extreme energy levels and inability to slow down, I didn't know what was going on. I only knew that I hated the state I was in. The excitement needed for the adrenaline rush I craved, was nowhere to be found. Not at the likes of the lumber yard, or anywhere else for that matter. Not even several more triathlons and a couple long distance obstacle and adventure races were able to fill that need.

I missed the simplicity and craved the insanity of Iraq. My insatiable appetite for all things had taken over. Just take one more step, I thought. Carry one more 2x4, and drink one more beer.

My bags were still packed. I was still on the run. Only instead of running from qunbala or an IED blast radius, I was now running from myself, the thoughts inside my own head, and the emotions I could not process. More importantly, I was now running from those who cared about me enough to challenge me into taking a deeper look at my current state of mind.

THIS SNIPPET covers the same period of time as my years at the lumber yard, but it includes my nemesis. Alcohol. Those six packs of beer I picked up on the way home turned my life upside down in a hurry. The introduction of my new favorite acquaintances, Samuel Adams, brewer patriot, and Jack Daniels, distiller of Tennessee whiskey, combined with my already unstable state of mind and ensured that my life would head in a generally downward direction.

Before reading on, I'd like to reiterate that I and only I, am responsible. I will never state that I am a victim of anything other than being human. No hands other than my own lifted the bottle.

It's time to meet Boozer. Normally he's a jovial skeleton, and always looking for a cheerful time to be had by all. However, Boozer has a slight allergy to alcohol. Sometimes when he sets out to simply enjoy himself with a drink or two… hundred, he breaks out in handcuffs.

PUSHING MY MIND WTH A BOTTLE

I have always enjoyed a good party. I enjoyed social drinking during college well before I was introduced to Boozer. Unknowingly, Boozer and I began a love-hate relationship shortly after my return from Iraq. At first, I loved him to be around because he really helped me calm the hell down. Booze(r) made me feel better. I just wanted to feel normal again and I drank in an attempt to do so.

Just as I had allowed my skeleton Adrenaline to take over my life, I also allowed Boozer to take over my life. One may conclude the results were far from the same. Adrenaline had saved my life during a few extreme instances. Boozer's influence on me, however, flew over like a lead balloon.

Boozer took over my life and I got arrested for Driving Under the Influence (DUI) around 45 days after Isaac was born. The fines cost Fi and me about $1500, and I spent a few days in the county jail. Over the course of the next six months, I was arrested again for another DUI. This next set of fines racked up in excess of $3000, and I spent fourteen more days in the clinker. I was lucky to have a driver's license at all, and I was also lucky to have kept those incidents from the Army. I have no idea how, but I managed to mostly maintain my radio silence to the military, pertaining to my alcoholic tendencies. This was partly due to the fact that many of my military fellows were in the same boat that I was in. Many of us drank in excess, together.

Meanwhile, at the VA triage room with no diagnosis, I was put on the back corner table with no benefits or treatment because my problems were that I just felt weird, had a few nightmares, needed to be busy all the time, and I drank too much. While I couldn't sit still, I was at a standstill with the VA. While others were learning to walk again after loss of limb, my body was whole. There were obviously more important people to be helping in the triage room. Over the first several years after my return from Iraq, there didn't seem to be any room for me in the VA medical centers.

I was putting Fi through every bit of hell imaginable. I cannot fathom what it must have been like to watch the person you care for throw himself down a hole, and just keep digging deeper and deeper. I was certainly the one causing all of the pain in this situation. For that I am forever sorry. Fi was unable to help me or comfort me in any way. She had a new baby to take care of, and she was tired. She has always been a great mother. Thank you, Fi.

> A side note. A few years later, my awful relationship with "She who shall remain unnamed" gave me a hint of the pain I put Fi through. That horrible relationship helped me understand how Fi must have felt. Over the course of eighteen months "She who shall remain unnamed" ate away at my trust in her and my bank accounts simultaneously, while I stood tortured by her side. It hurts watching a person you care for do things you could not imagine them doing. Fi watched me do that for four years.

Eighteen months after Isaac was born, Isaiah Tate Capell was introduced to the world. My second son is also one of the greatest miracles in my life. I love him, too, more than words can express.

Just as with Isaac, I was overjoyed with Isaiah's birth. Or at least I thought I ought to be. I still could not seem to capture the rightful happiness. I just couldn't experience the positive emotions that I should have experienced. Two and a half years after my return from the war, I was still a vampire with no reflection in the mirror, and emotionless.

Excellent at accomplishing all tasks at hand, I was great at helping Fi with the home, the chores, the bills, and the daily grind. Somehow I had managed to keep a steady paycheck coming in, but in lots of respects, I was like another child for her to attempt to take care of. I was completely checked out emotionally in regards to our relationship.

In addition to the alcohol, I knew something else was wrong with me, but nobody could seem to help me. My life was an absolute catastrophe and I could not seem to snap out of it. During a visit in which I attempted to explain my conundrum, a family doctor gave me a prescription for some anti-depressant medication. He warned me that if I didn't stop drinking so much the medication would not work. I took the meds for about a month, proving the Dr.'s warning to be correct. He was right, they didn't work while drinking. After yet another failure, just one of so many since my return from Iraq, came a self-diagnosis of alcoholism.

In another attempt at explanation, or rather a plea for help, a marriage counselor we went to stated that, "Alcohol was the elephant in the room." He explained that there wasn't any possibility of coming to a conclusion on the other things I may be suffering from, prior to dealing with the elephant.

In an effort to harness the elephant and ride him out of the room, I attempted all types of internal healing. Meditation, religion, Alcoholics Anonymous (AA) meetings, and exercise were among them. In an effort to make the elephant completely disappear from the room, I quit drinking for about six months, several times. During those periods I attended regular AA meetings, which was good for me. Meeting people who were attempting to change their lives was inspirational, but nothing seemed to change for me. I was actually more miserable during those stretches of so-called sobriety.

I enjoyed drinking. It provided an escape from the dreadful life inside my head and the reality of my own suffering. Over time, the reluctant elephant may have gotten as far as standing up, but that only made him larger than he was before. That elephant was not easily moved, nor was I.

Self, you're a stubborn asshole.
                              - Joel A. Capell

People who have a problem with alcohol are like a pickle. A pickle starts off as a cucumber, and at some point during its soaking in a brine mixture the cucumber becomes a pickle. It's very tough to discern the exact point when this happens, but once it does there is no possibility of the pickle becoming a cucumber again.

At some point during my own soaking in alcohol, I crossed a threshold from light into darkness. From enjoying Boozer all the time, I progressed to hating him, loving him... loving him, hating him ... and eventually just hating him. Just like the pickle, I cannot discern exactly when I crossed the threshold into destructive drinking, but I know I can never go back.

Fi soon asked me to leave the home as my destructive behaviors did not change. I was not a good father or husband at that time. I did not deserve my own children and now I will admit that with 100% certainty. I hated Fi for her decision then, but I thought it better for her and the kids if daddy "went away for a while" to get better. In retrospect, she probably saved my life by making that dreadful choice. I was spiraling out of control and she created the beginning of my personal bottom with that decision. Without her asking me to leave I would have kept digging. I'd have kept falling, possibly to my death or permanent incarceration. And God forbid may have taken her or our children with me.

While in Iraq and while performing most tasks in my life, I have always taken them to excess. I constantly tried a little harder, carried one more 2x4, took one more Advil, ate one more bowl of chicken noodle soup, and drank one more beer. Exceeding in nearly everything I attempted, drinking was no different. I succeeded in letting Boozer take me

189

exactly where he was supposed to take me. He took me to an altered state of reality and eventually to the floor. Alcohol was both keeping me from tearing my hair out, and was a large cause of me tearing my hair out. I really was an absolute mess. I didn't know if I was coming or going half the time.

Three years after returning home from Iraq, I was now living in the windowless basement of a widower's home in a suburb of Columbus, Ohio. Being newly separated from my family accelerated my downward spiral. Within a month of moving from my home, I uncalculatingly isolated myself from the world and had lost complete control of my life to Boozer. He and I spent many lonely nights on the floor of the bottom floor.

One night in my basement apartment in a drunken stupor, I fell to my knees in shock when I realized my complete desolation. My own driven lifestyle had gotten the best of me. In much the same way I had reacted to finding a bomb under my feet at the end of my Trailblazer mission, in that moment of desperation in the basement I'm not certain whether I cried, laughed, shuddered, screamed, or all of them at once. I may have hugged that bottle of Jack Daniels, I have no idea. I was completely overwhelmed by every aspect of my life. Despair pulsed through my veins to the rhythm of my palpating heart. Much like Trailblazer, I simply could not yield any more intensity. Boozer had seized me. I was broken. My mind left my present surroundings and I was no longer in that basement, no longer fighting, no longer running, no longer hiding, and no longer conscious of my current predicament.

My mind mixed up the happenings in Iraq with my current situation. Were the memories still rigged to the detonator? Thump, thump, pounded my heart. Had I been pushing that bottle of Jack Daniels with the dozer for the last mile? Thump, thump. Was my own life a secondary explosive device… thump, thump …meant to catastrophically detonate on me? Thump, thump. Was the first six pack of beer just a decoy? Thump… thump…

Overwhelmed by every question, every mistake, and every demand that was being made of me, I fully succumbed to the constant strain of not knowing how to deal with myself. My knees buckled under the 1000-

lbs. of mistakes and confusion I had carried with me since Iraq. I needed to go back in time. I needed to finish. What it was I needed to finish I didn't know. I was terrified, confused and utterly alone. I lost my family. I lost my ability to think. I had no more ability to reason. Leaning back against the bed in my room and the bottle of whiskey in my hand, as I had leaned against the bulldozer blade and my rifle, I again swayed helplessly back and forth. I had been defenseless and useless against qunbala. I was now defenseless against Boozer and useless to my family and to myself.

In that moment, a memory set like a timer rigged to an IED exploded in my mind. It brought tears to my eyes. I thought of Isaac and Isaiah's laughter as I tossed them into the air. Wrestling with them on what was once my living room floor, inside what was once my home. My own children barely even knew their Daddy. Their Daddy barely even knew his own children. I shattered into incapable pieces. Entirely alone. Life had taken me into its depths.

I swatted fruitlessly at a few Good Idea Fairies who were fully armed with suicidal ideas and ways to end all of my suffering. I was so torn, I was considering different ways to end the suffering permanently. Different ways to die. The evil Fairies swarmed around me, loudly suggesting that I finalize my misery. I stared blankly, at the static on the television screen rolling upward. Too intoxicated to physically move, I was lost.

Thump, thump, came the sound of my heart. Thump, thump. I was unaware as to how long the TV had been blank. Thump, thump. I just wanted to see myself in the mirror again. Thump, thump. I hated who I had become. Thump, thump. I had been through so much loss. Thump, thump. How could there possibly be more? Thump, thump. This will never... thump, thump... ever... thump, thump... ever end... thump... thump...

NO MORE ROPE, NO MORE HOPE

THE THOUGHT of suicide occurred to me multiple times while I was in this dire state. Those thoughts were whittled down into the specific way I would do it. Using one of my own pistols, I would end it all. According to the statistics all I needed in addition to my specific plan was two more things to complete this latest mission. The first was isolation. I was currently living in a basement, by myself. The isolation box had a checkmark next to it already. The second was being in an altered state of reality. Jack Daniels checked that box. My own deck was stacked, by me and against me.

Good Idea Fairies armed with a 9mm Beretta showed up knocking at my mind's door. After swatting a few of them away blindly, I knew an entire army of the evil and persuasive, life taking little fuckers would continue to haunt me. I was correct, they wouldn't leave me be. I pushed them away night after night. Running from them, alone and afraid, I couldn't trust myself and I knew it. Not having enough faith in myself to keep the thoughts of ending my own life out of my head is a pain unlike any other I have experienced.

"The River" by the Jompson Brothers (Featuring Chris Stapleton).
From "Live at The Shed in Maryville TN".
Courtesy of Smokey Mountain Harley Davidson.

https://www.youtube.com/watch?v=Kl5-Co74oAs

Had an Angel by my side
And the Angel had to fly
Took the Devil for a ride, for a ride
Put a pistol in my hand
And he whispered me a plan
Go ahead boy be a man, be a man

I was not going to let those Fairies win by taking part in any permanent solution to my problems. Needing a way to limit the possibility of suicide, during a brief moment of clarity, I handed over all my own personal firearms to my Father. He would keep them for the time being. With those pistols, I transferred the weight of my current world onto my Father's shoulders. We didn't talk about it much, but we both knew the reason I gave my guns to him. The love that he showed me by simply nodding as he placed them into the gun cabinet was something I hadn't felt in years.

At that moment I realized I wasn't actually alone. Reaching out to my Father for help opened the door to hope. Thank you, Dad, for being there for me through the disaster that I was. Thank you for taking that evil burden from my head.

BOTTOM

ON JUNE 8TH 2008 after nearly a year of separation from my family, countless empty bottles and nights with swarming Fairies, I hit bottom. In Newton Falls, Ohio, zip code 44444, while at a military school on military duty, I was arrested and got my final DUI.

I have no idea how I managed to avoid going straight to jail. The breathalyzer test I was administered showed nearly three times the legal limit for alcohol! God himself must have sent me a guardian angel, because the arresting Officer allowed one of my Army buddies from the school to come and get me. My truck, however, was impounded. I was certainly going to be discharged from the Army, and there was no doubt I'd lose my driver's license, which meant I would lose my civilian job as well. I had officially gone over the edge. But even that was not yet my rock bottom.

The next morning I called Fi and told her about my arrest and vehicle impoundment. The inevitable words "I want a divorce" scarred me instantly. They hurt so much I collapsed in the grass outside the barracks in which I had slept uneasily the night before. I was completely devastated. During all of the pain and turmoil, there was still hope of reconciliation prior to those words. When I heard those words, it horrifically registered within my brain that I was not going to be a father who was always with his kids while they grew up.

A soldier would sooner die than disappoint the ones he cares about the most. "My God… what have I done? My own children…"

With Fi's words, there remained no more rope to hang onto. All that lingered was a noose. I had dug all the way to my bottom and could dig no deeper in life. Only death could be below this point, and I wanted to die. This realization was well beyond all that qunbala had taken from me, and distinctly further than what Jack Daniels and the swarming Fairies had taken.

Sitting in the grass I realized that I had no more chances. I was losing my children as a result of my own actions, and that moment was the absolute lowest moment of my entire life. Rock Bottom.

Not another word was spoken. Radio Silence…

"No Joel! No more silence!" My guardian angel spoke to me while extending the rope one last time.

Devastated and shuddering in the grass, I hung on to that rope. Much like my last Trailblazer mission, begging and weeping uncontrollably, I turned to God the Father in heaven above. With what seemed to be the very last bit of strength I could muster, amid tears of absolute sorrow and gasps for air, I screamed out at the top of my lungs into the sky.

"PLEASE GOD… HELP ME!"

VII

Running & Chasing

3 DAYS AFTER being kicked out of the military school I was attending, and after having received word of my imminent divorce, on June 11ᵗʰ 2008, I voluntarily admitted myself into an inpatient Veterans Affairs (VA) facility in Brecksville, Ohio near Cleveland, for the next thirty days. As a veteran, I could receive inpatient care after my one year comprehensive care period had passed. Although my life was in shambles I still could not receive outpatient care because I didn't have a single diagnosis.

Again, I will never state that I am a victim. There are plenty of examples of veterans that never end up travelling down my personal route of destruction. Although there were factors that certainly "pushed" me down the path, my own actions had gotten me to this point.

One heavy foot in front of the other, weighted by all the burdens of my life's catastrophes, I walked desperately into a facility run by The Department of Veterans Affairs with the intention of staying there until I was better. Or until they kicked me out.

Jennifer, meet Adrenaline… for a second time.

ADRENALINE'S CURSE

The Army had begun to process the paperwork for my discharge immediately after my DUI was reported. A single DUI, anytime, is enough grounds for discharge. I had just been arrested while attending a military school, so there wasn't much of a chance that my career could survive the incident.

On the very morning I admitted myself, just prior to walking through the doors while outside on the grassy knoll in front of the hospital, I received a phone call about a government job I had applied for. Rick and I had never spoken before that phone call. I came completely clean with him during our brief conversation. Letting go of all inhibitions, I told him of my plans to spend thirty days inpatient at the VA Hospital.

When asked why I was going to stay in the hospital, I stated PTSD, even though I had no idea what was truly going on inside my head.

My name and the water cooler gossip headlines of my "soldier gets DUI while on duty" incident reached the Ohio National Guard State Headquarters where Rick worked the same morning it had occurred. A day later, Rick recognized my name on his job candidate list as the "DUI soldier". He contacted the Sergeant Major (highest ranking Non-Commissioned Officer) with whom I had been deployed in Iraq, in order to make an informed decision as to whether he should even make the phone call to interview me.

My Iraq deployment Sergeant Major spoke these words of forgiveness to Rick. "You don't kick a good dog while he's down." Thank you Sergeant Major, I will never forget that.

There were no reasons other than the Sergeant Major's words and the sincerity in my voice for Rick to do so, but at the end of our phone conversation, he asked me if I could begin working for him in forty days. That offer provided me with ten years of stable employment at a time when I needed it the most.

For some reason or another, the Army decided that they were going to give me another chance. I would be given an Article 15 (military disciplinary action), demoted from Sergeant First Class to Staff Sergeant and would be forced to transfer from my home in the Engineer Battalion to new job as a military logistician. I was going to have to become a POG (People Other than Grunts) if I wanted to stay in the Army. I felt blessed to have another opportunity, even though the awful decisions I made had rightfully expended all of them.

Although I had a deep hole to climb out of, I never let go of the rope. My eyes began to focus through the haze that was my life and I started to look upwards before walking through the doors at the Brecksville VA. There was nowhere else for me to go but up. I had lost my children, my wife, my home, my truck, my driver's license, my dignity, and the respect of all those meaningful to me. Rock bottom. But I wasn't going to let go of the rope.

"This is not who I am!" I thought to myself. But there was no doubt about where I was. I was about to walk into a hospital and beg for help. "Please God! Help me!"

The alcohol I had been consuming felt like it had little effect until I was unable to get myself off of the floor. I had no problem whatsoever letting Boozer take me there. When I was on the floor my body and mind were still. It was complete intoxicated bliss. It was an escape from reality which allowed full relaxation for both body and mind. There was no doubt I was abusing the liquid drug in order to make me feel better. Feeling better momentarily was no excuse for my actions. Nor was it a solution to my problems.

Once I crossed the threshold through those front doors I had a new focus. What do I do? How do I get help? Fix myself! What was wrong with me? I knew I had a drinking problem! But was there something else? I was a soup sandwich of a mess! Suicide fairies? More pain, more confusion! How does this end? My own life was just as chaotic as those last few jumbled sentences.

Over the next ten days I followed my doctor around the VA hospital. I'm not sure if he really took me under his wing. Truthfully, I wouldn't leave the man alone. I pleaded with him daily, hourly, every minute for something to do. If he would have allowed me to, I would have helped him with anything. File paperwork, take out the garbage, pick up the groceries, and balance the checkbook. Anything at all... please!

I sat in on every counselling session and participated in every service offered. I literally went to everything possible. I must have been a complete pest, insistently following him around.

"Please give me something to do Doc! I need to work Doc!" I begged him over and over.

I just wanted him to listen, but where would I start? I just wanted to be better, but what exactly was wrong with me? I had no idea. I just wanted to feel normal again, but had forgotten what normal even felt like. I just wanted to see myself in the mirror, and no longer see the dreaded monster I had become.

Here's an interesting tidbit about my true state of mind when I entered the hospital. About a week into my stay, someone called the VA and reported a veteran with a hospital wrist band running the streets of Brecksville, Ohio. It was now over three years since I had come home from Iraq, and I was still running every single morning, even while at the damn hospital! Drive on soldier! I wasn't wearing my hospital gown, but damn-it, I should have been. That's a much funnier image.

Blinders on, I was completely unaware of how ridiculous it was for me to be jogging while I was a patient at the VA hospital! I had to sign a disciplinary action form, and agree not to leave the hospital grounds again, or I'd be kicked out. Evidently Brecksville didn't appreciate hospitalized veterans on their streets. So instead, I ran around the hospital grounds eighteen times at 5:00 AM, every single day. And I'm sure I was running at a self-pressing pace.

Being so active was normal for me, so hyperactivity completely escaped me as a possible issue. It was all I had known for the past four years. But my hyperactivity was completely abnormal to the hospital and its doctors. When they finally began to take notice, they were simultaneously speechless and interested. I was not their typical patient.

Upon entry to the VA, I had to submit blood and urine samples in order to be tested for drugs. I wasn't even on any medications. Drug use has never been an issue for me. Doc told me later that he thought I was surely on some form of stimulant because my energy levels were off the charts. But when he had to write my disciplinary warning about leaving the hospital grounds to jog in the mornings, and also read reports of me sleeping soundly through the night, he began to wonder.

Was it adrenaline? Maybe his patient's adrenal gland had not shut off? Running the streets of Brecksville at 4:45 AM, yet sleeping soundly? The inability to sit still and maintain focus?

After following Doc around endlessly for two weeks he finally took some more blood tests, which confirmed his diagnosis. My adrenaline dam had broken, and the natural chemical had been gushing into my bloodstream since Trailblazer. He immediately prescribed me some medications for the next fifteen days, which slowed my hyperactive adrenal gland back down to normal levels.

Those pills worked their intended miracle. During my last week in the facility, I felt a sense of calmness flow over me.

To me, it was exciting to have a "cure". To the VA, I'm certain it was exciting to have provided that "cure". We were all happy! The VA had "solved" my case, and my doctor moved on to his next patient. After my adrenaline "dried up" I'd be discharged, so I was removed from the alcohol treatment program, and placed in the recovery ward.

Unfortunately, the damage had already been done to my marriage. The possibility of watching my children grow up from our home was gone. I had made some very, very poor decisions over the last three years. Those decisions were influenced by many more factors than just adrenaline. They had caused years of degradation and heartache for me and my family. I was eventually forgiven, but my actions are never forgotten. Just like the pink mist, and the lifeless eyes behind the burka, those poor decisions will also haunt me for the rest of my life.

SWING... AND A MISS - STRIKE ONE

As a separate part of my treatment at Brecksville, a counselor and I filed a VA claim for military service connected PTSD. We filed on day number two of me being there. In retrospect, filing a claim on the second day I was there made absolutely no sense whatsoever. I had not been at the hospital long enough to be diagnosed with anything. What grounds could I have presented to substantiate my claim?

A few months after leaving Brecksville I received the results from my claim in the mail. The experts within the VA had rightfully denied my claim for service connected PTSD. They had no grounds for awarding it because I unknowingly had failed to present any.

Having no idea of how the claims process was supposed to work at the time, I put my trust in the counselors who were hired to help me as a veteran. As I understood it, we had done everything correctly. And because I was denied service connection for PTSD, I thought I must be okay. I was newly cured from my adrenaline flood, and now the experts were telling me I didn't have anything else wrong with me. These people knew what they were doing... they were the experts. Who was I to question their diagnosis? I wanted to be "cured" anyway, so naturally I agreed with the VA's opinions, and we decided unanimously that I must be fine.

Let me reiterate the absurdity of filing that claim. Across the country, the VA is a part of ongoing investigations brought against them for countless incidents during this timeframe. Veterans were literally dying while waiting in line for care. The bullshit had even gotten to me. It wasn't as if I had gone to someone off the street to help me. Of my own free will, I walked into a hospital for veterans, which was run by the Department of Veterans Affairs, and pleaded to them for help!

"Someone, please help me!" were nearly the first word I spoke after walking through the doors.

A counselor, hired by the Department of Veterans Affairs, recommended that we file a claim with no evidence to back it up. I complied with the recommendation and we filed a claim, without submitting a single piece of medical documentation along with it. What in the hell were we doing?

Jennifer, it pisses me off to no end thinking about the absurd process that I went through. It makes me angry even to this day.

NO HOME & NO EMOTION

Shortly after my thirty-day stay, I became a resident at a shelter for veterans in Columbus, Ohio for seven days, at the recommendation of the VA. My personal belongings had been removed from the basement of the widower's home, so I had no home address. And my truck was in an impound lot somewhere in northeast Ohio. After paying an arm and a leg for impound lot fees, I stayed in my truck for a few nights, and then at the veteran's shelter. Then I stayed in a hotel for five nights, before moving into an apartment. I resided in a hospital, my truck, a homeless shelter, and then a hotel. I was homeless for more days of my life than I ever thought I would be.

What I didn't know was that even after coming down from the adrenaline flood and leaving the VA hospital, I was still unable to process the mental anguish I had been through. And because of that my anger levels remained high. The new adrenaline regularity did not automatically turn my normal emotions back on.

For instance, I knew I loved my children, but still wasn't capable of experiencing the feeling of love. Truly, it was almost as if I was incapable of positive emotions. Instances when normal would have been to feel happiness eventually ended up mutating into anger. Every emotion that attempted to find its way into my psyche ended up in feelings of anger. Just like the adrenaline, anger had also been gushing inside of me since Trailblazer. My hyperactivity had effectively masked the anger. And let's not forget about the elephant in the room having plenty to do with my current lack of emotion as well.

I can remember an instance during this time frame when I was watching a heart tugging movie with someone, and I literally broke down in tears. The person I was watching with became angry because I evidently had shown no emotion toward anything until watching this movie.

While I was deployed, I broke down over my dog Kallie, but negated the grieving process for my Grandfather altogether. Now I could cry over a sad movie, but could not feel the love I had for my children. And I could not show even the very simplest of positive emotions, like gratitude, in my day to day life.

Jen, I know you'd agree that I don't really "feel" things appropriately sometimes. I get "stuck" on things that make me angry even to this day. That makes me a jerk sometimes. The absence of positive emotions is unfortunately common among veterans. Compound me being an angry ass, sometimes, into not being capable of "feeling" anything, all the time. It really was like being a vampire with no reflection.

In retrospect, here's another example of my lack of emotions. Imagine listening to a loved one as they talked about accomplishing a lifelong goal. Most people would rejoice alongside the loved one because of their achievement. At the time, I didn't have any reaction at all, which made me an instant jerk to my loved one. And because I didn't have a positive reaction when I was supposed to, which was typically pointed out to me, I would eventually morph that positive void into anger, well after the conversation was over.

After the void morphed into anger, I became an asshole. It was kind of like my own personal BOHICA moment. The good would morph into bad, almost instantly. It was an awful way to exist, and I seemingly had no control over it because I wasn't even really aware it was happening. Add a little alcohol to the mixture... poof, an angry, drunk, asshole.

In a professional capacity, no one had ever asked me any questions about emotion. No doctor, therapist, social worker, etc., had ever asked me about my feelings, or my lack thereof. And I had never challenged myself about them either. I was completely unable to talk effectively or express myself about my experiences in Iraq, and how they had changed me. I had never really even attempted to think about Iraq. I wanted to avoid it, let alone talk about it. I had no idea where to even begin.

In a loving capacity, the people who cared about me the most were always given my best happy faced mask. I didn't do it on purpose, but I was able to fool them just like the audience members watching me speak Spanish in my A+ earning performances. I knew when I was supposed to "walk across the stage" and hug my children, but didn't properly feel the emotion that should have been attached to the action.

Truthfully, I didn't know what was wrong, so how could I explain it? In an emotional sense, I was definitely lost. But I wasn't looking for help from anyone who might hold a map, professionally or personally. Because I didn't realize I was lost.

At the Brecksville VA, we never even began to explore these emotional issues. So, the next VA doctor that looked at my medical file would see that I once had a subacute adrenaline problem, but nothing else. After Brecksville I was finally capable of being calm or relaxing slightly... but I was now an angry asshole, who really enjoyed Jack Daniels.

Not another word was spoken. Radio silence...

Through the process at the VA, I had recovered from adrenaline overload. It was a small but significant victory, taking place three long years after returning from the war in Iraq. For many more years I would continue to run from some of my skeletons, while simultaneously chasing answers from anyone who would listen.

THE NEXT couple years had their respective ups and downs. My life did thankfully continue, and I certainly had my struggles, just like anyone else. During the post Brecksville years there were many good times, but there were some bad ones as well. Taking everything into account, day by day I was managing to climb out of the hole I had dug myself into, and was living my life as normally and as inconspicuously as I could. When the Fairy demons told me that I could no longer climb for myself, I switched gears and kept moving up the ladder for my boys. I was triumphing, healing, seeing myself in the mirror, becoming proud of myself again, beginning to trust my own rationale, and becoming the father that I needed to be.

Even though I was healing internally, I had no business whatsoever being in any type of serious relationship. Especially with someone that was possibly more unstable than I was.

Jennifer, I know that you will never stray from our vows. This is an entertaining, if heartbreaking, story about someone that did.

THE AXE AFFAIR

"She who shall remain unnamed" and I had a short marital affair that started with a double edged sword union between the two of us, and literally ended with an axe. In early 2010 "She who shall remain unnamed" and I collided by chance and limped our way into an elopement gamble about nine months after each of us had finalized our own divorces. Writing this story will take the same amount of time as our entire relationship. Divorce paperwork was finalized in December 2011, before the relationship really ever started.

I was still emotionally blind and did not heed the warnings from my Mother about "She who shall remain unnamed". I was definitely lonely. I had been internally lonely for many years. Not being capable of being my own friend, I was in a very lonely place. And there was not a person on the planet capable of filling that void. I saw her cuteness, and outward persona, and before I really even knew who she was, we had tied the knot. Our relationship was destined for failure from the very beginning. It was a demolition derby, continuous wreck of a marriage, conceived for all the wrong reasons.

Let's skip everything about how downright wicked she actually was to me, and get to the fun part of this otherwise awful story.

I left "She who shall remain unnamed" for three months in the new home I had just purchased for us, in order to attend a military re-classification school in the Pocono Pennsylvania area. I had to become a POG. Through this opportunity though, I was making excellent money stateside, and was beginning to rebuild a little financial stability. Or so I thought. While attending the electronics maintenance school, some telltale signs of untrustworthiness were brought to light. Consequently, I whirled myself into a private investigator, and assigned myself to my case.

Sherlock Capell presents exhibit #1: signs of infidelity from "She who shall remain unnamed". And exhibit #2: several random and unexplainable disappearances of funds from my bank account. I knew something was amiss from 500 miles away.

Upon my return home from the military school, the suspicions I had were validated with exhibit #3: an entire new wardrobe for "She who shall remain unnamed". And exhibit #4: a newfound and out of the ordinary, sexy style of dressing.

Armed with the obvious deceitfulness, I confronted her about wearing new high heels to a workplace where she changed into scrubs and a pair of tennis shoes. The confrontation proceeded as expected with a complete denial from "She who shall remain unnamed".

Prepared for her denial, and quite proud of my Sherlock like abilities, I immediately presented the next bit of evidence in my case against her. Exhibit #5: phone and text message records that I pulled from our wireless phone company's website.

One unknown number repeated itself in those records over and over again. "No big deal," she said. "It was just a co-worker." She completely denied my allegations, again.

I have no idea why I tried to save the relationship with this clear evidence, but I did. Drive on soldier. Due to exhibit #2, the disappearance of funds, it was obvious she was stealing from me and I had more than just a hunch that she was cheating on me. In an attempt to "refocus" our relationship, I planned a weekend camping vacation for us in the Hocking Hills, Ohio area.

One week later, I took Friday off of work so I could pack for the trip. That morning I got in her car to retrieve the GPS navigation device and while doing so found exhibit #6: an electronic door key to a Red Roof Inn.

Oh shit! This was not going to end well. I knew that fact, but really wasn't feeling anything. I should have felt deceit, pain, and betrayal. There were innumerable possible emotions for the situation, but I felt nearly nothing concerning a cheating and lying spouse. Except anger.

It had been many years since I last heard it, but that hotel key instantly made my angry heartbeat come alive inside my head. Thump, thump. Knowing she would deny allegations. Thump, thump. Sherlock made a separate plan for confrontation. Thump, thump. On the back of the key was an advertisement for a Domino's Pizza. Thump, thump. I entered the pizza delivery number into my own phone. Thump, thump. And placed the hotel key back into her car's console. Thump... thump...

While disguising my obvious concern about what I had just found, I proceeded to pack for our trip. Tent, sleeping bags, air mattress, water container, plastic ground cloth, rope, folding chairs, iron skillet, Coleman cooler, and an axe to split wood. It was a large axe, with a three foot hickory handle. All the essential camping gear.

"She who shall remain unnamed" left for work around 10:00 AM. Shortly afterwards I hopped into my car and began driving in the general direction of her workplace with all the required camping gear packed in the hatchback of my sport utility vehicle. I knew that it was highly unlikely that this endeavor would actually have a positive outcome. But maybe, just maybe, I could put my suspicions from this morning to rest, and focus on the nice vacation I had planned for us. I wanted to try, and maybe, just maybe, "She who shall remain unnamed" did too.

The excessive behaviors I have had since childhood are certainly not always a good thing. One step further, one more try, one more act of forgiveness. Maybe she wasn't fooling around? Maybe she just wanted to look exceptionally nice?

Self, you are an idiot sometimes.
                                    -Joel A. Capell

At 11:00 AM sharp I called the phone number to the Domino's pizza which I had taken from the back of the hotel key, and asked where that particular franchise was located. Sherlock's new best friend, Google Maps, then presented me with a map and directions to the Red Roof Inn, located in the same Columbus suburb as the Domino's Pizza. I drove directly there, and it was at that Red Roof Inn where I found exhibit #7: her car in the parking lot.

"She who shall remain unnamed" was at that hotel, at that very moment. Realistically, I knew what was coming. I drove out of the driveway of my house knowing.

"Well, here we are? Now what, you idiot?" I sarcastically yelled those anger riddled words at myself. Even though I suspected this was coming... I had no idea what was about to transpire.

Thump, thump. "Shit! Ohhhhhhhhhhhhhhh shit!" Thump, thump. My heartbeat took over. Thump, thump. There was now absolutely no doubt in my mind. Thump, thump. My perceived notions had been confirmed. Thump, thump. There goes the neighborhood. Thump, thump. At that moment... thump, thump ...I got out of my car... thump, thump ...and lost my mind. Thump... thump...

I sent "She who shall remain unnamed" a single text message. "I'm outside," was all it said.

The guy she was with, whom I'll kindly refer to as "FuckYouGuy", moved the drapes just enough to peer around them. He saw me standing rigidly in the parking lot. He quickly shut them in an "Ohhhhhhhhhhhhhhh shit" moment of his own. Nice work Sherlock! I now knew which room they were in.

Keeping my dignity intact like any emotionally distraught but prideful man would do, I walked back to my car and pulled out the axe with the three foot hickory handle that I had packed for the camping trip.

Impulsively, I approached the door to the Red Roof Inn. Axe in steady hands, I was going to get through that door. If nothing else I was going to make those two awful human beings believe that their lives were about to come to an end.

The first impact from my axe to the steel framed door brought a single scream from within the room. The shriek made me smirk in a joyfully wicked way. I am certain there were more screams, but all I could hear after the first strike of metal was my own pulse race through my body.

Thump, thump. At the same pace my pulse was beating, I delivered the strikes of the axe to the door. Thump, thump. With my trusty lumberjack tool I let loose. Thump, thump. Powerful and revenge filled swings. Thump, thump. One swing for every dollar she stole from me. Thump, thump. One more swing for each of her cheating text messages. Thump, thump. I would get through that door. Thump, thump.

"Fuuuck," I swung the axe and raged aloud. "Yoooou," I swung again. "Guuuuuy!" I literally screamed each word aloud. To the beat of my heart and my swings, I named him appropriately.

I swung my axe in his general direction. Thump, thump. I swung my axe in her general direction. Thump, thump. I broke into a sweat of wrath. Thump, thump. Why me? I swung away. Thump, thump. "God-damn you bastards!" I screamed aloud. Thump, thump. I had already been through so much loss. Thump, thump. This will never… thump, thump… ever… thump, thump… ever end… thump… thump…

In a grunting frenzy, with one last swing for myself, the door finally swung inward and smacked loudly against the wall.

"She who shall remain unnamed" cowered in the corner of the hotel room, trembling. Her knight in shining armor had abandoned her and locked himself in the bathroom. I heard "FuckYouGuy" fearfully calling the police from inside the shower. Hearing that coward bastard cry out loud brought another joyfully satisfying grimace to my face.

From her perspective, I imagine peering at me in that instant from the corner must have been terrifying. Terrified of what I might do after witnessing what my powerful and persistent shoulders had just accomplished. Terrified, while thinking her head may be next. Between the sun, which silhouetted my stocky frame in the doorway, and the axe in my hands, I must have been a bone chilling sight.

I let the axe fall to my side, and it's now dull blade head hit the concrete sidewalk with a loud "clink". Still holding the handle in my right hand, and taxed from breaking through the metal door, I breathed deeply with each heartbeat. The only part of me that crossed the threshold into the hotel room was a couple drops of sweat that I shook from my forehead. My chest grew larger with each deep breath, and with each exhale it subsided. I simply stood there silhouetted by the sunlight behind me. Not saying a single word and not moving an inch.

Not another word was spoken. Radio silence…

After a minute of standing there and letting the intimidation factor fully set in, I awoke from my silent fury. Drive on soldier. There is no doubt in my mind that both of those terrified awful human beings believed that their lives were about to come to an end when I broke through that door. I had accomplished what I had originally set out to do, so I walked back to my car and returned the axe to the pile of camping gear in the hatchback.

I grabbed my checkbook out of the glovebox and walked calmly into the lobby of the hotel. Still sweating and breathing heavily, my voice remained calm. Just loud enough to be heard over the soft elevator music in the lobby, I asked to speak with the manager on duty. Because honesty is always the best policy.

It really was like a scene from the movies "Pulp Fiction" or "Tombstone". Mass destruction followed by elevator music and calmness in the empty hotel lobby, right around the corner.

"Sir, I'm going to need to buy an exterior door for one of your hotel rooms."

In the next two minutes I told the manager everything that had transpired over the last two hours. From my awesome Sherlock detective work phone call to Domino's pizza, all the way through "FuckYouGuy" locking himself in the bathroom.

The manager looked at me first with confusion, then sorrow, horror and slight laughter when I told him the jackass was probably still locked in the bathroom. We walked around the side of the hotel so he could confirm that I had in fact axed through his hotel door. The manager then asked me if the sirens we heard off in the distance were headed our way. I confirmed that it was my belief that they probably were, as I had overheard the frightened conversation from within the bathroom while I stood at the room's threshold.

"You're going to write me a check for the door right now?" asked the manager with a hint of understanding to my situation.

"Yes Sir. That is my intention. If you can give me a cost for the door and its installation, I'll write you a check right now." I handed him a check just as the first police car arrived.

The first officer on the scene asked me for ID and I handed him my wallet. I was told to sit on the curb of the sidewalk and then was handcuffed. I calmly obliged as the police took statements from everyone involved. I overheard the hotel manager tell the officer exactly what I had just told him, in entirety.

The police evidently couldn't believe that I didn't inflict any physical harm. I repeatedly overheard them ask everyone if they were hurt. My guess is that if I had hurt anyone in any fashion, the officers would not have had the liberty to be as gracious as they were about to be.

Finally, the two love birds drove off separately, escorted by the secondary patrol cars, leaving a single police officer on site. He was the rightful owner of the wrist necklaces currently against the small of my back. The hotel manager was also standing next to us.

I never got a good look at "FuckYouGuy". I'd have loved to have stared him in the eye, and had a single opportunity to just jump in his general direction. Even with my hands restrained, I'd have figured out a way to make him retreat one more time in my presence. I still don't even know his name. For brevity, I've always referred to him as the aforementioned expletives. "Coward Mule Feces Asshole Bastard Piece of Shit", also suffices.

After everyone else had left, as he un-cuffed my hands, the young officer said that he saw my Military ID in my wallet while looking for my identification. The hotel manager then mentioned that he happened to be a Desert Storm veteran, and that more than anything, he'd simply enjoy telling the story of what had just transpired. It was a story for the ages, from his normally monotonous midday shift.

Veterans share a brotherhood unlike any other. Police Officers fit right into our brotherhood mentality.

The three of us chatted about "The Axe Affair" for a brief period, while I rubbed my wrists back to life. Handcuffs suck! Hopefully, I will never experience them again. The officer was going to let me go, and the hotel manager was not going to press any charges. My debt had been paid in full, and I had obviously had a far worse day than either of these two gentlemen. After a couple minutes, the warrior's code of "duty first" called the officer to return, and he asked me if I was going to be alright?

Was I going to be alright? I pondered his question only briefly. Even if I was not, I certainly wasn't going to tell him otherwise. I was about to put this entire incident in my rear view mirror, along with "She who shall remain unnamed".

It was now 2011, and the officer didn't need to know that I hadn't really been alright since mid-2004. He didn't need to know that I was about to be going through my second divorce, that I'd been arrested four separate times, had multiple DUI's, spent thirty days in a VA hospital, been fired from a job, lost my driver's license twice, lost military rank, and had spent a month incarcerated if you add up all the stints in county jails. He didn't need to be told that I had spats of uncontrollable anger, and that I had put a few holes in drywall with my fists. He didn't need to know that I wasn't even really sure if I was capable of expressing love, and certainly not of feeling it. He positively didn't need to know that if he let me drive away right now, I was going to stop at the nearest bar and attempt to drink the first half of this day into oblivion. After what had just happened to me, I needed a drink. I needed all the drinks. But he didn't need to know any of that.

"Yes… yes Sir. I'm going to be fine." I believed in the words I had spoken. Sometime in the future I was "going to be fine". But was I currently alright? Hell no, I wasn't. I stretched the truth to save myself from the moment.

It was about 3:30 PM when I stopped at a local watering hole that day. I proceeded to tell my story of "The Axe Affair" to the bartender and several bar patrons.

"God-damn, son, you've sure had a rough one," was the bartenders reply as he poured me a tall beer and a short whiskey. I downed the whisky and motioned for him to pour another. He poured them long for me, all night long.

I basically drank for free, well into the wee hours of Saturday morning. I ended up sleeping in the back seat of my car, across the street from the bar, under a sleeping bag that was packed for a camping trip that I was never going to take. Normal people don't sleep in their cars. Normal people don't break down doors with an axe. I knew that those things were weird. But I didn't care.

"She who shall remain unnamed" took two years of my life, and completely stomped me back into my hole. Just when I was beginning to finally enjoy my own company again, she ripped my life from beneath my feet. She hurt me, there is no question about that.

Today, a smirk of enjoyment crosses my face every two weeks when considering "The Axe Affair". I collect that grin in the form a direct deposit into my bank account from "She who shall remain unnamed". She pays the debt she owes me from every single one of her paychecks. "She who shall remain unnamed" stole over $15,000 from me while I was at the electronics school for the Army. She is required as part of the divorce settlement to pay me back in entirety. Sherlock Capell did an exceptional job presenting a separate fraud case that was written into the divorce settlement. The Judge stamped it approved, no lawyer required. That evil wench would be ordered to pay me back every two weeks for about nine and a half years. I hope she remembers "The Axe Affair" too, every… single… time.

Sometimes life has a dreadfully charming way of working itself out.

VIII

The Gift

THE BOTTLE was put back on the shelf immediately after that appalling relationship disintegrated into court paperwork, and I refocused once again on my children and myself. I had another deployment (my second) coming up in about a year, and was actually looking forward to it. My life was moving forward prior to leaving for that second deployment.

BbO - YOUR CHAPTER

A year or so after "She who shall remain unnamed" began to pay me $30 biweekly, I was feeling a different type of loneliness. There was a yearning for honest companionship that began to take ahold of me. I needed a better half to compliment my newly sturdy arm. I really didn't like the idea of creating an internet dating profile and throwing myself out there to the masses for the superficial photo viewing possibility of finding true love. But I did it anyway.

After what seemed like countless days of viewing profiles thrown at me as possible dating prospects, a country girl with a degree in accounting and long, blond, beautiful hair flew into my heart. In her online photo she had propped herself up in a tree. She was stunningly beautiful, had two children about the same age as Isaac and Isaiah, and was currently working as some sort of financial loan officer.

Jennifer, you flew into my heart from a photo taken in the branches of an oak tree in Papa's front yard. There, you instantly created a permanent place inside my mind. A desire to fill that place with memories, rather than expectations, took over.

We exchanged text messages through the dating website a few times, and eventually set up a date at a Max n' Erma's restaurant outside Columbus. Honestly, I cannot remember anything about the conversation that day. I was completely lost in the sparkle of life within your eyes. I'm sure we spoke about our kids, our families, and work and leisure activities. All I wanted to do was schedule the next date. And we did. On day number one, you created a Jennifer memory that nested comfortably inside my head.

Unfortunately, I was headed to Kuwait in a few months for my second deployment. We broke things off for obvious reasons, and went our separate ways for about fourteen months without communication.

Just after meeting you, my second deployment in 2013-2014 was truly a blessing for me. It gave me some much needed financial security. It reemphasized my own responsibility for myself and for life in general. That deployment helped me find some of the stability for which I had been searching. Midway through that deployment, I no longer had to constantly climb out of that seemingly never-ending hole I had created. I had finally reached some sort of plateau.

While the first deployment to Iraq completely destroyed parts of my life, that second deployment helped save it.

I returned from Kuwait in early 2014, and shortly afterwards was looking for an Army colleague's phone number in my phone. She was also named Jennifer. I happened across your name, listed as Jennifer M. Before I made the call to my colleague, I placed a hopeful phone call to you. When I heard your voice, you instantly settled directly back into that nest in my head. We scheduled a lunch date for a week later, on the grass outside of the library in Dublin, Ohio.

I had to do a double take upon seeing you again. I remember every single thing about the way you sparkled in the sun's warm rays that afternoon. You had propped yourself up on the hillside, reclined on a blanket. You were wearing a khaki knee length skirt and a white button up shirt with cuffed sleeves. Your golden hair hung down around your shoulders and shimmered as it flowed over the curves of your body. You had flipped your shoes off in the green grass, and were reading a newspaper folded into a quarter of its original size, through a pair of baby blue framed glasses. I was absolutely smitten.

The greatest date of my life transpired that afternoon. We shared hours of stories and strawberries, after a lunch of sushi from a full picnic basket. It was the most beautiful of warm Ohio spring days. My heart fluttered with the birds as they flew around preparing their own nests for spring hatchlings. Shortly after that beautiful day, and our first long kiss, the lovely Jennifer was replaced by an even more stunning "Babe" in the nest belonging to you. You had become "Babe".

Those who know me would say that I am somewhat of an unwavering and immovable object. I know you'd agree with them. I am not certain I would have made it this far if I wasn't so stubborn. The turmoil I have been through over the years makes the heartaches of normal life seem trivial. I fit naturally into a sturdy role as the rock to your wavy shores.

Your beautiful mind is as exciting to me as the ocean is blue. Your zest for life and ability to throw caution to the wind is the perfect complement to my sturdy and sometimes overly rational way of thinking. We are the perfect fit. As I write this love letter home to you, I simply cannot wait to smell the fragrance of your perfume. And to hear your voice as you tell the stories about the inevitable excitement of your days. Your days are always filled with excitement in my mind's eye.

Becoming a permanent fixture in your life is one of the greatest gifts I've ever been given. By giving myself completely, I have been given more than ever fathomable. Allowing me the opportunity to help carry life's little weights, and the promise held in our once separate worlds, is both awesome and a great responsibility that I love dearly. We each brought our own bags to the scene, filled with clothes, separate families and homes, heartache, and newfound happiness. What I love about it all is that I now have a partner in life that I can confide in, and trust completely. No borders, no walls, everything is entirely open between us. That is an amazing feeling.

Hearing the word "yes" from your lips when I asked you to marry me will never be replaced by a better word.

You are that blue ocean. Wavy and fierce at times when you need to be. Strong enough to make this tired soldier stand tall when by your side. You are simultaneously as tranquil and beautiful as a Sanibel Island sunset. You are a risk taker, and within you resides the innocence of a children's book. This specific book, "The Belly Button Book", by Sandra Boynton, is about a beach full of bare-bellied hippos, including one baby hippopotamus who can only say "Be-Bo" when referring to his own belly button. It is a book that we both read over and over again to our own children's delight.

I have gone through yet another change because I now have you. That stunningly beautiful "Babe" who propped herself on a hillside, has brought an even greater, inner beauty than I ever thought possible. When we first met, you were "Jennifer" in the nest within my head. By touching my soul, you became an even better "Babe". And now as my wife, my confidant, my better half, and my best friend, you have become the best. The most beautiful woman I know is you! BbO.

"Die a Happy Man" by Thomas Rhett,
from the album "Tangled Up", 2015

https://www.youtube.com/watch?v=w2CELiObPeQ

If I never get to see the northern lights
If I never get to see the Eiffel Tower at night
Oh if all I've got, is your hand in my hand
Baby I could die, a happy man

Occasionally, my skeletons have reared their ugly heads, resulting in stress and strain in our relationship. Throughout all of that, it has been obvious to me that you, like me, will never give up on us. That is something that I will never take for granted, but only as a blessing.

My "Beautifully Beautiful Ocean", I'll forever be your rock. BbO, you are one of the greatest gifts in my life.

IX

The Truth & The End

FINALLY truly happy in my own skin again, it's no small surprise that chronology correlated directly with BbO. You make me happy, Jennifer.

Changing gears for this next letter, while continuing with the chronology, let's say hello to another skeleton. Her name is Burka, and she has dead, unresponsive eyes. She doesn't blink or show any emotion, she only stares. Her blank stare pierces deeply into my soul.

LIFE IS A SERIES OF DEPLOYMENTS

In one of his acts, comedian George Carlin said that, "Life is a series of dogs."

> *I love every dog I ever had. ... In my lifetime, I have had me a bunch of different dogs. Because you do keep getting a new dog don't you? ... That's the whole secret of life. Life... is a series of dogs.*
>
> -George Carlin

For those of us who love our canine friends, these statements do seem to hold true. However, for a soldier, life is a series of deployments.

Imagine leaving home and investing an entire year of life fighting for and supporting something with so grand of a purpose it is almost incomprehensible. Then returning home only to realize that despite everything accomplished, every sacrifice, every long day, it was still not enough. That's what soldiers do. A deployment can be a most daunting task, and an equally daunting realization of unfinished business is often present afterwards.

There is no doubt in my mind that after a first deployment, a soldier believes that their next one will have a similar or elevated level of purpose, mixed with a bit less hesitancy. The military almost "hooks" soldiers that way. Like a largemouth bass chomping irresistibly on a spinnerbait, soldiers chomp down tightly on irresistible unfinished business, and the chance to support an enticing global cause once again.

Most veterans respond admirably to duty's call when they are asked to deploy again. It's what we do. But then we think to ourselves, "why in the hell am I here?" the entire time we are deployed. This is another example of how sarcasm is born in a veteran.

Utopian war is the epitome of an oxymoron. After putting forth my maximum effort in Iraq, there was not a single possibility that I would wrap everything up before leaving. Years after my experience there, part of me truly wanted to go back to work on unfinished business.

When the opportunity arose, I chose to go back to the Middle East in 2013-2014. And choosing to go back actually worked for me. I came home from my second deployment a rejuvenated man, having found fragments of my persona that had been lost for a very long time. In retrospect, I found those bits of humanity only because they had been absent for so long.

Go one step further, make one more effort, carry one more 2x4, pound one more nail, and go on one more deployment. Drive on soldier.

Even though I had to leave our home and your side, Jennifer, I would say that you'd agree that my third deployment in 2017-2018 has had some blessings attached to it. It has certainly created stability for us financially, and was great for my overall health.

This time however, I would run off to a foreign land in support of something I wasn't sure I even believed in anymore. The Army had called me, and rather than permanently retire, which was my only viable option to the deployment, we decided together that I should go. The spinnerbait lured me in and I chomped down one more time.

With regards to the global cause of fighting terrorism, and being part of the "tip of the spear", my Iraq deployment will forever outweigh all the others. However, I did find something of great personal value while I was deployed for a third time.

In-between CTEF missions, and exercise sessions at the gym, the first part to the valuable findings happened when I sent a draft of "Radio Silence" home, while I was not home.

> Jennifer, while adding to these letters in Kuwait, I wanted to somehow involve you. The additions to them and their transformation into "Radio Silence" were a very large part of my deployment experience. I wanted you to be able to experience this part of my life with me. I was pondering publication and wanted some insight from the woman I trust the most.

Like when Joel "Paul Bunyan" Capell chopped down the giant tree for a bridge as a child, when I made the decision to include you in this process I had my blinders on again. My tunnel vision prevented me from seeing the possibility of overwhelming you. In retrospect, even though we had discussed them before, bombarding you with stories of alcoholism and suicide Fairies was a horrible idea. Not because you didn't want to know or understand the entire story, but because of my absence from your side at the time. I obviously had no intention of hurting you or making you worry. But I did, and I am very sorry.

My decision to share these experiences in detail with you while I was 6700 miles away made me realize that, no matter the amount of time between qunbala and the present, the fact is I am indeed a hardened man. Because of the War on Terror I have learned to deal with some extremely abnormal experiences in my life. Similar to becoming used to bullets flying and no longer running for shelter, the emotion and pain involved within these letters are now second nature to me. But they are not second nature to most, and not second nature to you.

I failed to see the obvious discomforts these letters might bring you because I lived them, and had been writing about them for ten years. You, however, had not. I presented them to you during a time when I was not there to give you a hug and answer any of the multitudes of questions they have raised. It was not the correct time to do so. Thank you for understanding my intent rather than fixating on the results.

The second valuable finding was revealed one Sunday afternoon when I went into Kuwait City to purchase some things for our family. My purpose for the day was to purchase a few small presents to send home to you and the kids, and my overall enjoyment of a much needed day off. For soldiers, these trips into the city were a very nice escape from the daily grind. They were a well-deserved chance to spend a little hard earned money and enjoy a foreign culture.

In Kuwait City, it was normal to see women dressed in the full, black burka style dress walking through the mall or the streets of a marketplace. A burka completely covers a woman in black cloth from head to toe, with only a one inch slit for her eyes to see out into the world.

I cannot explain why it happened. I only know that it did.

Seeing the burka clad women on that Sunday afternoon took me immediately back to Iraq. The one inch slits in their facial garments that revealed eyes peering eerily out into the world brought with them a fit of internal anxiety. Suddenly, I was full of all the original fears of kneeling in front of qunbula and sweating profusely just before pulling the wire.

My heartbeat took over. Thump, thump. A self-made sound that had been absent for years, pulsed loudly once again. Thump, thump. I could hear nothing else. Thump, thump. But I could see her… thump, thump …the woman in full burka… thump, thump …with dead, unresponsive eyes. Thump… thump…

Seeing those women brought back the memory of the dead woman in full burka dress, the woman who had died as a result of my ordering a barrage of Operation Vigilant Guardian firepower upon the building in Iraq. From thirteen years ago, my skeleton Burka had arisen and she was currently alive right before me, strolling among the other women.

Seemingly immune to the wounds we inflicted, she was now walking. Her dead walking corpse stepped slowly toward me. In my mind's eye, she also had blood running down her leg making her dress stick to her right side. Time seemed to stop all around Burka. She moved slowly.

And she creepily just stared at me with her lifeless eyes. Her stare pierced me, and Iraq began to swim into my soul. Her dead, unresponsive eyes haunted me, once again.

The actual women walking toward me made eye contact briefly. As a good Muslim woman would do, they immediately and shamefully looked downward as they had been taught. But not Burka. She did not blink or flinch as she moved among the other women. She did not look down in shame or fear. With her connecting gaze it was as if she transferred every horror, every loss, back to the forefront of my mind.

From Trailblazer to losing my children, the alcohol and the adrenaline, swarms of suicidal Fairies, death and destruction, never grieving for my Grandfather, and losing my mind to "the one that didn't go off". They all loaded themselves up into a battering ram and connected with my sternum with the brutal blow that was her stare. The breath was forcefully knocked from my lungs, and I heard my heartbeat pound.

Her stare only lasted 20-30 seconds, but it was difficult for me to focus on my actual surroundings for the next five minutes. And it was obviously not the type of thing that I wanted to bring up in conversation on a day when everyone was supposed to be having a nice afternoon relaxing. But images forever stamped into my memory were undeniably foremost in my mind once again.

Thump, thump reverberated the sound of my heart into my ears. Thump, thump. Unaware of how long reality had escaped me. Thump, thump. No! Not again. Please go away. Thump, thump. I had already been through so much. Thump, thump. How could there possibly be more? Thump, thump. This will never… thump, thump …ever… thump, thump …ever end. Thump… thump…

After Burka disappeared and my mind returned to reality, I had to sit down for a few minutes. Luckily everyone else took a short break as well, so I didn't have to explain myself. The black cat and I had once again crossed paths.

Not another word was spoken. Radio silence…

I had experienced a flashback to a moment in Iraq that had occurred thirteen years prior, and it made me break into an uncomfortable sweat in the middle of a populated and peaceful shopping mall. The anxiety of the moment was not completely debilitating, but it certainly was impactful. I had a painful experience because my skeleton friend, Burka, decided she'd like to resurface. I sat, clammed up, and was silently fearful that I was about to head down another path of self-destruction.

I temporarily lost my mind one more time during that trip into Kuwait City. The second time was while we were in the van on the way back to the base. Again, burka clothed women crossed my path, this time on the road directly in front of us while we were stopped in traffic. Horns blaring, 117 degrees, traffic completely stopped, a claustrophobic's nightmare, I wanted to get out of the van. But she was out there, and I was once again paralyzed by her dead, unresponsive eyes.

Burka had resurfaced, and she decided to stay for a while. I don't know why she wanted to stay, only that she did. For the next few weeks, she was always on my mind. Burka obviously bothered me, but she wasn't what flipped the switch for me to seek help, again.

After years of searching for answers, I still had something unnatural happening inside of me. Thirteen years after the fact, I was still screwed up. And that realization exhausted me, and pissed me off. What turned the page for me to seek help was becoming angry again. After Burka resurfaced, I morphed back into the asshole that could not express or feel any emotions, except anger. And I could not seem to flip the switch in order to turn Burka or the anger off. I was stuck on full angry, again.

"Why was I still running?" While writing my frustration in these letters I brainstormed, and began to list thirteen years' worth of my cries for help.

This next blurb is what I actually wrote during that session. My unedited thoughts, mostly consisting of questions to myself, are as follows:

I have cried out… haven't I?

Several times I have filed claims with the VA but have been denied repeatedly? I've walked into three separate VA facilities complaining of everything from alcohol addiction to depression? Nightmares have resurfaced for short periods of time? I told counselors about them. Skeletons have resurfaced for short periods of time? And I also told counselors. I started a couple different VA therapy programs? Expressed blatant distress in my life to counselors? Spent 30 days inpatient at the Brecksville Veterans facility where I ran the streets at 4:30 in the morning… like any good soldier would? Went to three local private counselors seeking help in small town Ohio through military funding sources? Actually called Military One Source (a full service phone number for veterans) and utilized some of the benefits? I have been arrested four times, sent through court systems, sat in front of judges, and been thrown in jail repeatedly? I've been in handcuffs five times? I have taken down the door to a hotel room with an axe? Was court ordered to go through alcohol rehab where I sat in daily sessions with social workers? Been on reporting and non-reporting probation for years of my life? Been divorced twice and had multiple DUI's? Thoughts of suicide? A plan for suicide? Guns loaded for suicide? Had to present my case for each of those things on my personal criminal record to a government investigator in order to obtain my security clearance?

Then I began to think of the people who knew about these things. Who were the people that had actually listened to my pleas? Who had heard me? Again my unedited thoughts:

Counselors, VA reps, psychologists, therapists, sociologists, doctors of medicine, prison guards, judges, police officers, probation officers, investigators, and social workers. None had actually taken notice? I was just another number passing through their systems. Hell, after all of that life destruction I wasn't even diagnosed with anything but a drinking problem? I wasn't even on a single medication? I had no continuing care from anyone anywhere? To this day I can't list a single name of even one of the "professionals" that I have seen over the last thirteen years? I don't even have a name. In thirteen years, not even one... single... name? Who the hell was listening while I was talking, expressing, screaming, drowning, suicidal, falling? The answer is... no one.

After writing the previous paragraphs, my heartbeat took over like it had so many times before. I was so angry.

Thump, thump. I was the one who had self-admitted. Thump, thump. For heaven's sake? Thump, thump. A facility for veterans? Thump, thump. I walked in the front door and pleaded for help? Thump, thump. I begged for help! Thump, thump. And don't even have a damn name? Thump, thump. Maybe I answered all the questions... thump, thump ...incorrectly every single time? Thump, thump. I obviously still had issues... thump, thump ...that I have never dealt with. Thump, thump. The black cat! Thump, thump. Her dead, unresponsive eyes! Thump, thump. She walked right in front of me? Thump, thump. Right here in Kuwait? Thump, thump. I saw her? Thump, thump. This will never... thump, thump... ever... thump, thump... ever end... thump... thump...

"Please God! I am tired of this! I've made up my mind. I don't want to run anymore."

Raising the surrender flag is difficult for a veteran. But, it was time for me to end the radio silence.

JEN, I AM PROUD TO BE A WARRIOR! I am also proud to be a man with enough intellect to reflect on my warrior actions. These warrior actions have had consequences that have touched those dearest to me, in both positive and negative ways. While on my third deployment I had already overwhelmed you with these stories. And now I was having Burka flashbacks, was angry for many reasons and also angry for no reason at all. It took me about twenty days of escalated internal anger before I finally sought the expertise of a professional.

I can finally write down the name of someone who listened.

DR. IN

During all of my previous therapy sessions, and in all of the various venues, I had failed to present my case every time. There are only two possible explanations to that conundrum. Either I wasn't talking, or the people who I was talking to were not listening. No... I know I was talking, but maybe I wasn't saying the right things? Maybe they were listening, but not comprehending the full issue? With sincerest honesty, I believe it was a combination of the two.

With regards to my part of that equation, I didn't want to be sick. Personally, I didn't want to admit to my problems. Even when I had previously attempted disclosure, I had never given a single person the entire story. There's thirteen years of story to tell, how could I? I wasn't even sure what to say, or how to begin the conversation. And let's face it, these things are not part of an everyday conversation. Radio silence.

My first appointment with Dr. In was on a Saturday morning in late August 2017. After sitting down in his makeshift deployment office, I prefaced with, "I don't really know how to get this process started, so I'd like it if you'd just listen to me. Would you please allow me tell you a story, Sir?"

Dr. In agreed to listen and I began to recite portions of these very letters to him from memory. From Trailblazer, thirteen years ago, to Burka, a few weeks ago, I told my story from these letters, in detail. It took up most of the hour of time that was allotted for our first appointment. He just sat there and intently listened to me, until I was finished. Something no one had ever done before.

After ensuring that I had finished speaking, Dr. In calmly responded with his own analysis of the last fifty minutes. "So, you'd like to work through some PTSD issues?" he asked. He had obviously been listening.

"Is that what I have?" I questioned his diagnosis. "I've never actually been diagnosed with anything. Although I've tried this before with counselors, I've never really made it very far in the process."

> Jen, as a direct result of reciting parts of these very letters, the discussion and the healing began. Writing these letters to you, and then reviewing them aloud with Dr. In, directly started the process of bringing my story full circle.

Over the next five months, the good Dr. and I dove into my mind every Saturday morning. We dove like the C-130 airplane did when Pawpaw and I landed in Iraq. This time, however, I was not on board as a terrified passenger clinging to the cargo netting. I was inside my mind as the confident pilot, who maneuvered among the paths of memory. I took all commands from Dr. In, who manned the ground tower.

Slow is smooth and smooth is fast. Many thoughts were slowly uncovered and deliberately dissected. Many memories were categorized. Many emotions were sorted. Much thought and care was intentionally taken. Every miniscule and stressful detail we uncovered was handled with ultimate care and understanding.

Uncovering the details was only part of the process. Much like a Trailblazer mission, now that we had found an IED, we had to deal with it.

Putting my engineer schooling to work we opened up new patterns of thought, detonated pathways for new roads, and built foundations for exploration. We bulldozed over many of the fears and anger enticing emotional reactions which I had stored over the last thirteen years.

During flight maneuvers, we twisted and turned, sometimes losing control. There were moments of weightlessness and some hairy landings. We even fired the M61 Gatling style rotary cannons. Soldiers neutralize right? Together we neutralized a few of the roadblocks I had created.

I was required to laboriously think and rethink about Iraq and how it had affected my thought patterns and processes. I was forced to test the painfulness within my mind and regain command of these thoughts. Forced to make amends with, and shake hands with Adrenaline, Qunbala, Boozer, and Burka. I was made to look into Burka's eyes and see them in a way that I never had before. What was once lost had been found behind doors that were not even present prior to our weekly expeditions. It was a very interesting time to be the pilot inside of my mind.

Dr. In saw in me what so many had failed to perceive before. I'd like to take a moment to thank him for following through to the very end, and for just simply listening to me. I am a better man now that I am able to finally file away those thirteen year old folders, full of unfinished business. Unlike the countless others that came before him, I will remember his name.

In early 2018, after my last appointment with Dr. In, he handed me a very important piece of paper with a diagnosis of "Chronic Post Traumatic Stress Disorder" on it.

And here we are… February, 2018. In less than 30 days I will be home from my current deployment.

Burka, and the lingering skeletons may never go away permanently, but I am now able to see them in a different light. Maybe the next time Burka surfaces, I'll be able to smile at her and she'll wink back at me?

Maybe the next time I go to the VA, I'll be understood as a struggling veteran because I finally have the correct piece of paper?

Through those sessions and these pages, I have gained awareness and some closure, at last. I have certainly turned the pages on the "stuck point" that was my life, and have ended the radio silence found within.

No doubt, one of the toughest decisions in this entire process was simply pushing the "Enter" button on a keyboard. "Pressing Enter" in order to publish "Radio Silence" was full disclosure pressed one step further. Drive on soldier. Regardless of how hard it was to press that button, the message within these pages was able to help me, so maybe it will help someone else.

SOME THINGS you just know. From time to time a person just has a gut feeling that there is more than meets the eye.

Camouflaged within the camouflage in the title on the cover of these memoir letters, is the word "DONE". Take a look at the green letters on the cover, you'll see it. After many years of service to our great nation, I believe it is time for me to come home and permanently unpack my bags.

COLD HARD TRUTH & THE END

Despite the fact that we are the strongest military on the planet, we have changed our tactics from those of a feared Rottweiler into those of a well-loved Labrador retriever. On January 1st, 2005 the U.S. military changed its Rules of Engagement policy, and the implementation of a "police state" began in Iraq. Since then, like a Labrador, we have intimidated by barking loudly, and then have proceeded to lick the retreating terrorists in the face while they reorganized under a new name for jihad.

I wanted to explore how the loss of the Rottweiler edge in the American military has affected the War on Terror. I'm not sure I ever found the answers for which I was looking for. However, I did find these grim and grisly facts, which speaks a cold hard truth.

The first part of my inquiry required that I find out how much money the U.S. taxpayer had spent on the War on Terror since 9/11/2001. The following excerpt is from a Watson Institute, Brown University paper, entitled "Costs of War". The monetary truths are as follows.

> *As of August 2016, the U.S. has already appropriated, spent, or taken on obligations to spend more than $3.6 trillion in current dollars on the US Wars in Iraq, Syria, Afghanistan and Pakistan and Homeland Security (2001 through fiscal year 2016). To this total should be added the approximately $65 billion in dedicated war spending the Department of Defense and State Department have requested for the next fiscal year, 2017, along with an*

additional nearly $32 billion requested for the Department of
Homeland Security in 2017, and estimated spending on Veterans
in future years. When those are included, the total U.S.
budgetary cost of the wars reaches $4.79 trillion. (Crawford,
2016)

It took me a minute to catch my breath after reading about the obscene amount the U.S. taxpayer has fronted for the Global War on Terror.

For the second part of my inquiry, I wondered how many terrorists had been sent to meet their 72 virgins since Sept 11th, 2001. It's a brass knuckle look at Samuel Colt effectiveness, from a hardened man. There were various numbers listed through many articles and studies. I chose to go with an average of the numbers at 74,000.

At a total cost of $4.79 trillion dollars, and a Samuel Colt effective rate of 74,000 dead terrorists, an equally disturbing monetary value follows. $64.7 million U.S. dollars was the cost afforded to each bad guy we have laid to rest. According to those figures, I should currently be worth $180 - $240 million dollars.

These bleak figures are a straight laced, down to business, reality check representation of this war and the effectiveness of the United States military as a police force rather than a killing force. Politicians stabilize. Soldiers neutralize. As soldiers we are not currently allowed to do so effectively.

The figures also represent how the slightly twisted thought process works inside my head. The years of not being able to unpack my bags have hardened me and turned me into a somewhat colder version of my former self. There is no amount of money that can be associated with the humanity that has been taken from me. Truly, there is no amount of money that can be associated with a human life, period. I feel slightly evil for even contriving such a comparison of figures. But the numbers do not lie.

I'm tired. I'm tired of fighting with BOHICA moments, and drained from the continuous warding off of the Good Idea Fairy. I'm exhausted by the needless and constant screwing's from the Green Weenie. I am tired of the military constantly changing the rules on me. I'm also tired of deploying every three to four years.

> Jen, that deployment rate is minimal compared to some veterans. Personally, I have completely missed a quarter of my children's lives due to military obligation. There are many veterans who can say they have missed half, or even more. We are tired.

It pisses me off that military recruits are still being sold ideas like, "One weekend a month, and two weeks a year." Or, "Sign up for 100% paid college tuition." And my personal favorite, "Collect retirement a year early for every year deployed."

Soldiers who have been in the Army for any amount of time understand that there is a ton of fine print associated with each of those promises. No soldier performs just one weekend a month anymore. It's not 100% of college tuition, it's 100% of some made up number of what tuition "should cost", but never actually does. And nearly everyone knows that spending a year deployed rarely adds up to a full year towards early retirement. Those recruiting bullshit lies, full of stipulations and fine print, would be severely punishable under Asshole Law.

Soldiers want to know why? Soldiers just want to go home! At least this soldier does!

Things like needlessly smashing my EyePro and watching Riot Reaction Training on PowerPoint slides, have sent me completely off the deep end. Before I am forced to drink all the flavors of kindness Kool-Aid through excessive "Mandatory Resiliency Training" (MRT, yes that's a thing), it's time for this Rottweiler to exit while my head is still held high, and while I still have my edge as a man.

Thump, thump. Stop stealing our edge America! Thump, thump. As a country… thump, thump …we do not want the alternative! Thump, thump. As a soldier… thump, thump …I do not want the alternative! Thump, thump. Leave us be! Thump, thump. And let us be proud!

Thump, th… STOP!

Dear Heartbeat,

I would like to genuinely thank you for maintaining your enduring beat over all the years we have known one another. There have been some tough times for both of us, but together we have weathered the storm. Hearing your "thump, thump" reverberate inside my head was the only thing that kept me going during a few of those moments. I will always have the need for you to be my constant companion in life, so please keep beating for both of our sakes. Frankly, things would have been quite bleak without you around.

The reason I am writing you this letter is to talk to you about our skeleton friends. I know they have been frightening us for years now. So before you get all worked up and start thumping uncontrollably, I can assure you that we have no need to be afraid of them anymore. Give them an honest chance, for us.

It has been very nice at times to block out the noise of the world with your constant beat. But, by identifying our skeleton friends in a different light, we have managed to turn a page in life that you and I were stuck reading over and over again. Together, all of us have laid a few things to rest. So let's not get so worked up about them anymore.

I understand your desire to lock out the fears. It was difficult exploring what is contained in these letters, and it may also be difficult to share those memories with others. But full disclosure within, and full publication without, will definitely be freeing. Doesn't it sound absolutely wonderful to no longer live in radio silence!

Although I will always need you around, I am no longer angry, so there is no need for you to beat as loudly. Hearing the entire world around us will be quite refreshing now that we can see ourselves in the mirror again. You have my word that I am not ignoring you. I am simply no longer allowing you to be the only thing that I hear reverberate within my head.

Sincerest thumping,

-Joel

X

Fond Memories

TWENTY PLUS years as a soldier have given me many fond memories intermingled with the darker war stories I have packed away in my duffel bags. I'd prefer to wrap things up on a much lighter note, so the next few letters are about various humorous and silly adventures across the globe. They don't follow any specific timeline, just a fun one. You will enjoy these stories, Jen. I enjoyed living them.

GNOME

Growing a moustache is a rite of passage for soldiers. As a social experiment on your own appearance, a moustache has almost become an unwritten requirement on deployment bases across the world. Come on! How can a soldier carry a loaded rifle, but not grow a moustache? If you don't have the nuts to attempt it, then what kind of man are you? There are no tangible rewards for those taking the plunge to the dark side and attempting a moustache. But the entertainment value is priceless.

The amount of entertainment value created during the inception stages of a moustache is downright amazing. Not quite like viewing Phantom of The Opera live on Broadway or witnessing Niagara Falls for the first time amazing. But, more like Uncle Eddie slipping on the ice in the driveway, and spilling his beer all over himself amazing.

Seeing a new moustache grow in the mirror daily, and watching a few friends fail miserably at the attempt, can only bring one thing to light. That thing is laughter. The idea is truly sophomoric if you think about it. So, as soldiers we don't think about it, we simply do it.

For decades U.S. soldier grooming standards have required the removal of all facial hair except what resides on an upper lip. Military regulation requires that little spot of lip hair to adhere to a ridiculous amount of guidelines. Just like anything else military, even a simple moustache has published regulations that seem to take the fun out of things. No pencil thin, no handlebar, no curly. We must maintain a groomed and neat appearance. The list of requirements in Army

Regulation (AR) 670-1 describing the correct appearance of a moustache literally goes on for several pages. Just in case there are questions about absolute conformity to the standard, there are even hand drawn black and white pictures of blank faces with moustaches. Yes, I say again, there are pictures of proper military moustaches in an Army Regulation.

Some men simply cannot grow one at all. Normally this would be considered a blessing as it would require less shaving. These considerations, however, are of no consequence during a deployment. A "deployment stache" is grown with no regards to actual presentation or self-esteem. In fact the more hideous a mustache, the higher regard it holds among our fellows. Even those who can't grow a healthy stache are highly encouraged to participate.

During the endless wearisome days of a deployment, moustache growing is normally just a simple and fun way to pass a couple months of time. In this instance, a few of my longtime friends and I decided to take the phenomenon of the deployment stache to the next level.

Upon sprouting a 10 day hideous moustache, well on its way to a great upper lip beauty, one of my friends printed a self-made, single page certificate, and hung it on his bunk. We'll call him BB. On the certificate, he ordained himself as an Honorary Minister of GNOME.

G.N.O.M.E. Certification of Ordainment

for

B. B.

an

Honorary Minister of the

"GRAND NOBLE ORDER OF MOUSTACHE ENTHUSIASTS"

BB called the GNOME Court to its first order of business the evening after his certificate appeared. All who had a moustache were invited. There were nearly 25 of us in attendance. Upon pounding the gavel,

Fred, a fellow moustache enthusiast, proceeded to read the following GNOME bylaws.

Know ye that entry into the Grand Noble Order of Moustache Enthusiasts requires strict adherence to the policy mandated by this sacred document. The only requirement for membership is the growth of a moustache. Any deviation from the requirement listed herein shall subject the member to chastisement of the most extreme sort, and public shaming. The offender shall be looked down upon through the glory of our majestic lip enhancers till the deficiencies have been corrected to the satisfaction of the Board Of Overzealous Bureaucrats (BOOBs). Unequivocal compliance to the regulations established herein shall be maintained, lest the offending member be cast into the general population and receive no further complimentary remarks from the whole of this organization, regardless of the efforts made to maintain and further enhance the regal nature of his (or her) impressive follicular accumulation.

-Fred Ullmann

Laughter and diplomacy ensued. With BB presiding as President, we elected a Vice President, a Treasurer, an honorary Moustache Judge, and four BOOBS. The BOOBS had to be elected in pairs, of course. And because we were currently located in the middle of Arabia, we even elected a czar, a "Moustache Czar". Our Czar, a man of great moustache-ular fortitude, was Vietnam era fighter pilot hero and triple ace, Robin Olds.

It became the middle finger I couldn't raise in PR photographs. The moustache became my silent last word in the verbal battles I was losing with higher headquarters on rules, targets, and fighting the war.

-Robin Olds

How could GNOME not elect a man with quotes like that one?

Our GNOME organization even applied for endorsed moustache club membership status via several "official" groups online. Yes that's actually a thing. Though we never heard back from the various places we sent application letters to, I am certain that moustache enthusiasts worldwide rejoiced as their fellows smoked cigars, played cards, and drank nonalcoholic beer together in the Middle East. We gathered henceforth, on Wednesday evenings, as part of the Grand Noble Order Of Moustache Enthusiasts.

Moustaches are very common in the Middle East, and most men have some sort of facial hair. By the time I left the Middle East, on that specific deployment, I actually fit in with the natives. The local citizens sometimes spoke Arabic to me while I walked among them in the local marketplaces. Of course I had no idea what they were saying, but I did look like one of their sons.

I have since taken the GNOME trademark, and my own impressive follicular accumulation to every one of my military deployment locations.

Me fitting in with the locals.

Even the family got involved in GNOME.

WHILE GROWING moustaches overseas on my second deployment, my unit was also charged with "taking care" of many of the units located on the Arabian Peninsula. We supplied them with nearly everything needed for their overall war effort. We even supplied a few boats.

For years, the Army has struggled to obtain repair parts for these old boats. Millions of dollars have been spent on contracts for their upkeep. Jennifer, they are still floating in the Middle East today.

BOATS & MARGARITA'S

While deployed in 2013-2014, we supplied the warfighter with beans, bullets, financial services, contract monitoring, general supply, ammunition, etc. We managed tasks as simple as delivering mail and monitoring chow hall contracts, all the way to the difficult task of obtaining repair parts for five old U.S. Army vessels. Part of the deployed war package in the Middle East, was an Army Boat Battalion, whose mission was the transport of goods via sea to various ports around the Arabian Peninsula.

These five boats were a giant PITA (pain in the ass) for everyone involved. They were non-tactical delivery vessels that were highly visible to Commanders. Because playing in the sea is typically a job for the Navy, these Army boats were on all the Commander's radars, even though they had very little operational impact on the total war effort.

At the time, there was not a lot of fighting going on in the Arabic portion of the Middle East. Most of the battles had shifted to the Taliban in Afghanistan. President Obama was even attempting to get us out of Afghanistan. The U.S. military Generals in our area of operations needed to have something to focus on, and part of what they chose for their efforts were the five Army boats.

These boats were similar to the 2-3 children in a class of forty that the teacher spends 90% of their time scolding and reprimanding. Our school administration's principal, a two star general, Major General 'Keepafloat' ordered us to "keep those boats afloat". If I didn't know better, I'd say those boats threw themselves on the floor in childlike temper tantrums, lashing themselves about when they were asked to do something. They were breaking down all the time. They really were a giant PITA!

It was my unit's mission to review and appropriately downsize all of the current military contracts that were in place. Even though the American footprint had subsided within the Arabian Peninsula, the flow of American taxpayer's dollars had not. General Keepafloat wanted to cut spending by a third or more with regards to contracts. He was right, we currently only needed two thirds of the original overall supplies. In our area of operations, the Army had downsized when compared to a year prior.

As soldiers, we often witness firsthand a certain level of absurdity in military spending habits. This downsizing request was just the opposite! It was both an interesting and fruitful endeavor, which sought to save the taxpayer millions.

Since the boats were in every PowerPoint presentation, for every General Keepafloat briefing, it was natural that my unit was mandated to concentrate effort into cutting the boat's overall costs.

Repair parts for standard Army equipment were typically ordered through an automated system called SAMS (Standard Army Maintenance System). Boats, as you might imagine, were not so standard to the Army inventory. The boat's nomenclature (military title) wasn't even in the SAMS system. An item must first exist within the system in order to request parts for it, and SAMS didn't recognize the boats.

SAMS was in the process of being replaced by a new global system that would include the boats, but this future fix didn't help our current predicament. The boats were currently being repaired through a competitive bidding process. The contracting process was also a giant PITA, and because of it, the boats were very, very expensive to maintain.

My longtime friend BB happened to be a SAMS and an overall maintenance expert. He was truly the very best at his craft, maintaining Army equipment. In addition, I was the SAMS operator for the Ohio National Guard state headquarters. Together, we had all the skills necessary to input the boats into SAMS, I just needed some confident coaxing from my friend.

After talking with him about General Keepafloat's request to cut boat expenses, BB told me that he could: "Load a boat into SAMS, and order it a margarita mixer."

"Margarita's you say?" BB's claim had gotten my attention and it didn't take him long at all to get me to jump. Somehow, he is always successful at getting me to commit to ridiculousness.

I asked BB if he would testify to margaritas in court. Meaning, would he be willing to tell General Keepafloat? Before he slipped and said yes immediately, he asked for ten days to test his theory.

Giving proper credit where credit is due, BB was the mastermind behind the plan. I was simply going to help him MSU (Make Shit Up), and assist where I could. Eventually, I'd be the one to present our findings to our Lieutenant Colonel boss. If BB and I succeeded in getting the boats into SAMS, our Lieutenant Colonel would consequently be considered a rock-star in General Keepafloat's eyes. The truth was that we had no idea how we were going to accomplish putting a boat into SAMS. MSU…?

MSU pertains to instances where a soldier doesn't really know what he's talking about, but needs to camouflage that fact. BB and I were flying by the seats of our pants on this one. We were going to have to MSU. BB talked me into the challenge, like the instigator that he is, and I presented the idea to our Lieutenant Colonel. Who really only wanted the tools to make himself sound smart when he presented the idea to General Keepafloat.

Our Lt. Colonel was none the wiser after my brilliant MSU dissertation. He gave us the ten days to test our theory after I sold a few ice cubes to the unsuspecting Eskimo. And then he pitched the idea to General Keepafloat. Shit-sticks! There was no turning back now.

As long as I could MSU, and make it sound good, neither of them would know the difference. They believed in us, therefore they believed in our idea.

After about twenty phone calls, BB and I found that a boat could actually be input to SAMS. That good news was immediately followed by a resounding, "Absolutely not!"

According to the contractor data file gatekeepers, putting a boat into SAMS was more difficult than the process was worth. The file gatekeepers were 7-8 hours behind us in time zones, and echelons above our reality. We were guys who essentially just wanted to fix a boat. We wanted a solution, not a complete history of the SAMS program. And with a new system which would fix our problem on the way, the answer from the gatekeepers was to wait. We hit roadblocks one through 34 within our first three days of attempts.

Many would have simply stopped there. "It can't be done", was a convenient explanation. BB was not going to give up so easily. I am fairly certain he was more interested in ordering a margarita mixer than actual parts for the boats. Nonetheless, he wasn't about to give up.

I never really understood why the boats weren't in SAMS to begin with. Weren't they equipment, owned by the Army? The "Good Idea Ferry" vessel must have left out its sister vessels on purpose.

We needed to invent some way to put these boats into SAMS. Upon further examination, we found a piece of equipment called a Fording Vessel that we could load into SAMS. It was not actually a boat, but it was close in title. We decided to give it a shot and loaded our first boat into SAMS as a Fording Vessel. Serial #, engines, communications equipment, and all the other components entered were from the actual boat. The title of Fording Vessel was the only thing we needed for SAMS to allow us to load the actual boat parts. It worked.

Now we had to find a solution to the second half of the problem. Could we actually order legitimate parts for a boat that was loaded into SAMS as a Fording Vessel? In the mind of the SAMS, we would essentially be trying to request windshield wipers for a canvas tent. The boat parts we needed were not the same as Fording Vessel parts. And SAMS had certain foolproof mechanisms built into its systems to make sure a $750,000 M1 Abrams tank's turbine engine couldn't accidentally be ordered for a generator.

BB explained that he knew of a few back doors that would trick SAMS into allowing us to order our windshield wipers. It turned out that BB was correct. We could in fact do just that.

Now, for the culmination of a man's dream. "Margarita Mixer" was not on the official Department of Defense procurement parts list. But our Army chow halls ordered "Blender, Food Processors". Why the hell shouldn't he go for it? BB was on a roll, and there was no way I was going to get in the way of his internal satisfaction. Even if I had to take an ass chewing for it, I wasn't about to be the one to take down his dream.

On the morning that we stood in the principal's office, BB told General Keepafloat that he had, and I quote, "Loaded a boat into SAMS and ordered it a margarita mixer".

He presented General Keepafloat with the margarita mixer, and received an impact award that he gets to wear on his formal dress uniform. BB had accomplished the impossible. We turned a blind eye to the naysayers, and got the job done. And as a result the boat repair contract was completely terminated, which saved the U.S. taxpayer hundreds of thousands, possibly millions of dollars.

"Hammer", "BB", "Chief", "Silk", and me, all on a boat.

AFTERWORD

Over my years in the U.S. Army, I believe that I have fought valiantly for freedom from oppression, and for the people of the United States to live and to have the choices that they deserve. I hope that someday, our actions will afford the people of Iraq and the Middle East the same choices, though history may dictate otherwise.

Those years have taken their toll on me as a man, a father, a husband, and a soldier. I have had some humanity taken from me, but have had countless opportunities to give my humanity to others. For that I am forever grateful. The Army has given me a secondary purpose to my life, and many, many things to be proud of. There is no doubt in my mind that I would do it all over again.

Making sense of my PTSD has been both an incredible and tiresome thirteen year journey. Being able to identify and categorize each thought, each reaction, and to place each experience into its respective manila folder in my mind's filing cabinet is a very reassuring and peaceful end to this tedious adventure. It is certainly the beginning to another one.

Jennifer, now that we have gotten here together, I hope these letters help explain some of the reasons why I am the way I am. Soldiers want to know why. Wives also want to know why.

Most soldiers eventually realize that the larger, worldly purpose they are in search of is actually found within their own home. I have found that purpose. Her banner is Family, and she goes by the name Jennifer.

Dear Jennifer, this is how I got here.

Come to me, all you who are weary and burdened, and I will give you rest. Take my yoke upon you and learn from me, for I am gentle and humble in heart, and you will find rest for your souls. For my yoke is easy and my burden is light.

- Matthew 11:28-30

SSG Joel A. Capell, B. Co. 216th Engineer Battalion, Iraq 2004.

REFERENCES

Christopher M. Blanchard and Carla E. Humud. "The Islamic State and U.S. Policy". *Congressional Research Service.* February 2017.

Kenneth Katzman and Carla E. Humud. "Iraq: Politics and Governance". *Congressional Research Service.* March 2016.

Kenneth Katzman. "Kuwait: Governance, Security and U.S. Policy". *Congressional Research Service.* November 2017.

"United Airlines Flight 93". Wikipedia contributors. *Wikipedia, The Free Encyclopedia.* Web. 27 Jan. 2018.

"Bush Doctrine". Wikipedia contributors. *Wikipedia, The Free Encyclopedia.* Web. 28 Dec. 2017.

Jacob Brooks, "Texas First Lady". *Killen Daily Herald.* January 3, 2016.

Scott Stump, "Hug Lady Dies". *Today.* December 25, 2015.

"First Battle of Fallujah". Wikipedia contributors. *Wikipedia, The Free Encyclopedia.* Web. 27 Dec. 2017.

Neta C. Crawford. "Costs of War". *Watson Institute, Brown University.* September 2016.

Made in the USA
Columbia, SC
15 August 2018